Marketing and Public Relations Practices in College Libraries
CLIP Note #34

Compiled by

Anita Rothwell Lindsay
Eckerd College
St. Petersburg, Florida

College Library Information Packet Committee
College Libraries Section
Association of College and Research Libraries
A Division of the American Library Association
Chicago 2004

The paper used in this publication meets the minimum requirements of
American National Standard for Information Sciences–Permanence of
Paper for Printed Library Materials, ANSI Z39.48-1992. ∞

Library of Congress Cataloging-in-Publication Data
Library of Congress Cataloging-in-Publication Data

Marketing and public relations practices in college libraries / compiled by Anita Rothwell Lindsay.
    p. cm. -- (CLIP notes ; #34)
 Includes bibliographical references.
 ISBN 0-8389-8295-6 (alk. paper)
1. Academic libraries--Public relations--United States. 2. Academic libraries--United States--Marketing.
3. Library surveys--United States. I. Lindsay, Anita Rothwell. II. Series.

 Z716.3.M285 2004
 021.7--dc22

                    2004012376

Printed on recycled paper.

Printed in the United States of America.

08 07 06 05 04   5 4 3 2 1

TABLE OF CONTENTS

INTRODUCTION   1

CLIP Note SURVEY RESULTS   5

SELECTED BIBLIOGRAPHY   13

CLIP Note Survey   17

MARKETING AND PUBLIC RELATIONS DOCUMENTS   29

ANNUAL REPORT   31

Plattsburg State University of New York   33
Feinberg Library
Plattsburg, New York

EXHIBITS AND EVENTS PLANS   43

Goshen College   45
Harold & Wilma Good Library
Goshen, Indiana

FUNDRAISING PROPOSAL   51

University of Maine at Farmington   53
Mantor Library
Farmington, Maine

MARKETING CAMPAIGN   57

Goucher College   59
Julia Rogers Library
Baltimore, Maryland

MARKETING PLANS   67

Scott Community College   69
Scott Community College Library
Bettendorf, Iowa

Suffolk University   82
Mildred F. Sawyer Library
Boston, Massachusetts

MISSION STATEMENTS   103

Bowdoin College   105
Bowdoin College Library
Brunswick, Maine

University of Colorado   114
Kraemer Family Library
Colorado Springs, Colorado

POSITION DESCRIPTIONS   125

Arkansas Tech University   127
Pendergraft Library
Russellville, Arizona

Goshen College   128
Harold & Wilma Good Library
Goshen, Indiana

Swarthmore College   129
Swarthmore College Libraries
Swarthmore, Pennsylvania

PROMOTION PLANS   137

Drake University   139
Cowles Library
Des Moines, Iowa

Southern Oregon University   143
Southern Oregon University Library
Ashland, Oregon

PUBLIC RELATIONS PLAN   149

University of Florida   151
George A. Smathers Libraries
Gainesville, Florida

STRATEGIC PLANS   165

Creighton University   167
Reinert Alumni Library
Omaha, Nebraska

Goucher College   179
Julie Roger Library
Baltimore, Maryland

CLIP Notes Committee

David A. Wright, *Chair*
Leland Speed Library
Mississippi College
Clinton, Mississippi

Christopher B. Loring, *Lead Editor*
William Allan Neilson Library
Smith College
Northampton, Massachusetts

David P. Jensen
Van Wylen Library
Hope College
Holland, Michigan

Liz Kocevar-Weidinger
Longwood University Library
Farmville, Virginia

Jean Lacovara
Bryn Mawr College Library
Bryn Mawr, Pennsylvania

Jennifer Phillips
Chesterfield Public Library-Midlothian
Midlothian, Virginia

Brian Rossmann
Montana State University Libraries
Bozeman, Montana

Gene Ruffin
Gwinnett University Center Library
Lawrenceville, Georgia

Marcia L. Thomas
Ames Library
Illinois Wesleyan University
Bloomington, IL

Ann Watson
Denison University Library
Granville, Ohio

Corey Williams-Green
Albin O. Kuhn Library & Gallery
University of Maryland, Baltimore County
Baltimore, Maryland

CLIP Notes

The *CLIP* (College Library Information Packet) *Notes* series is published by the College Libraries Section of the Association of College and Research Libraries. The series allows small and midsized academic libraries to share information on practices and procedures they have implemented to address common issues or problems. The goal of the series is to address significant issues facing college libraries and to provide valuable assistance to them in establishing and refining their services and operations.

Each *CLIP Note* is basically comprised of three components: (1) a review of the literature and an analysis of survey results; (2) information gathered from surveys sent to participating libraries; and (3) sample documents (e.g., policies, procedures) submitted by the surveyed libraries and pertinent to the particular *CLIP Note* topic. The survey data and analysis, along with a brief review of the literature, suggest trends and/or general policies and practices in college and small university libraries, while the documents provide examples to those libraries developing policies and "flesh out" the survey results with specific examples of current practice.

Publication of *CLIP Notes* is done under the editorial direction of the *CLIP Notes* Committee, a standing committee of the College Libraries Section of ACRL. The Committee selects and approves each *CLIP Note*s publication project, or, as needed, selects compilers from a pool of applicants. Compiler(s) work most closely with the *CLIP Notes* Committee Chair and a Lead Editor, a member of the Committee, who acts as a liaison between the compiler(s) and the Committee and who facilitates the editorial process.

The Committee has developed a pool of libraries that have agreed to respond to *CLIP Notes* surveys and to supply documents for reproduction in *CLIP Notes*. These libraries serve institutions with enrollments between 750 and 7,000 students that are designated as Baccalaureate I or II, or Master's I or II in *The 1994 Carnegie Classification of Higher Education* (Carnegie Foundation for the Advancement of Teaching, 1994).

Further information about the *CLIP Notes* series is available at the Committee's web site:

http://www.ala.org/ala/acrl/aboutacrl/acrlsections/collegelibraries/collpubs/clipnotes.htm

INTRODUCTION

OBJECTIVE

The purpose of this marketing and public relations survey is to discover the following information: (1) Is the process formal (planning activities and written policies in place) or informal (on-going, day-by-day activity)? (2) What are the elements of this activity? (3) Who is involved and what resources are available? (4) How effective is the effort?

This *CLIP Note* provides current data and sample documents as examples of marketing and public relations practices in academic libraries. According to the Association of College & Research Libraries (ACRL) *Standards for College Libraries* regarding services, "The Library should establish, promote, maintain and evaluate a range of quality services that support the college's mission and goals."

What do we mean by marketing and public relations? A review of the literature indicates the terms marketing and public relations are generally used interchangeably (Smykla 1999). The following definitions clarify the two terms:

"Marketing is the management function that identifies human needs and wants, offers products and services to satisfy those demands, and causes transactions that deliver products and services in exchange for something of value to the provider" (Cutlip 1994).

"Public relations is the management function that establishes and maintains mutually beneficial relationships between an organization and the publics on whom its success or failure depend" (Cutlip 1994).

The literature implies "librarians do not promote library services well and often are reluctant to borrow from the private sector..."(Sass 2002). Some librarians believe they do not do marketing, but all organizations perform marketing-like activities whether or not they choose to call it marketing.

PREVIOUS SURVEYS

In 1985, Vikki Ford, a public relations executive, surveyed 48 state university libraries to determine the extent of academic library public relations. Her questionnaire was designed to answer the following questions: (1) Did the library have a PR program? (2) What elements comprised that program? (3) Who was responsible for its operation? (4) How effective was the process?

Ford identified three trends. First, 40 of the 41 respondents said they conducted some form of publicity, but only 17 reported planned PR programs. Second, 33 believe their programs to be moderately effective. Third, the high response rate indicated a high interest in PR programs.

In 1999, the Association of Research Libraries (ARL) published *SPEC Kit 240, Marketing and Public Relations in ARL Libraries*. The survey's purpose was to identify the relationship between marketing and public relations and funding. The Association looked for answers to the following questions: (1) To what extent have North American libraries developed organized programs in the areas of marketing and public relations? (2) Who holds positions in these areas? (3) What impact do these programs have on library funding?

The ARL survey revealed libraries with marketing and public relations activities rate them as important and effective. Most libraries (79%) reported increased funding because of marketing and public relations activities. These activities consisted primarily of distributing printed materials and employing public relations professionals.

WHY MARKETING AND PUBLIC RELATIONS

Librarians must prove the value of their library to the institution's decision makers. Marketing and public relations practices provide the means to accomplish the following objectives: to qualify for diminishing financial resources, to compete with other information service providers, to assess user needs and to satisfy those needs, to increase awareness of library resources and services, to communicate the value of the profession, and to subscribe to the professional standards and guidelines established by ACRL.

Funding in a sluggish economy is a primary reason to reconsider librarians' involvement in marketing and public relations activities. Wilson and Strouse assert in their *Marketing Tips for Information Professionals*, "Your world continues to change, however. You can no longer afford to be merely a librarian. You are an information professional and the manager of a department. You run an expensive and important business unit. You operate in a business environment, and therefore, you must play by the rules of business. The number one rule of business is that *everything relates to the bottom line.*" (Wilson & Strouse 2002)

Competition for institutional monies is not the only threat to the viability of libraries. The Internet and Web has removed the barriers and restrictions to information collection and retrieval. According to The Factiva 2002 White Paper Series: *Free, Fee-Based and Value Added Information Services*, "Sixty-two percent of information seekers believe anything is available on the Web."

Librarians know seasoned researchers do not rely on the Internet to meet their information needs. Research by Bates reveals "Two-thirds of the publications used most often by knowledge workers (professional information seekers) either do not have Web sites or do not make their material available on the Web for free."

Librarians are also proponents of information literacy. They direct patrons to high-quality information from credible resources available in and through the library. As a valuable institutional resource, academic libraries provide user interface tools to aggregate and speed up information searches. Quality resources, value-added services and the knowledge of librarians are fundamental to the success of the organization. (Bates 2002)

An awareness of the competition for funding and an increase in the use of the Internet and Web does not lessen the reality that many nonprofit organizations resist marketing. Some do not acknowledge their services and resources need marketing. When the need for marketing is recognized, it is often seen as a 'necessary evil,' not as a means of moving the organization forward into the future. (Mahady 2002)

In today's sense of the word, marketing means determining user needs and satisfying those needs. It need not compromise ethics, services or budgets. "Marketing is necessary to help nonprofits promote their values, accomplish their mission, and develop increased resources to address a wide range of compelling concerns. Your marketing message should reflect the heart and soul of your work." (Mahady 2002)

Although a lone voice in the stacks may still cry out, "I'm a librarian not a marketeer," the perception of marketing and public relations in academic libraries is changing. Many professional organizations now offer marketing resources and services. In April 2003, ALA launched the ACRL "@ your library" campaign. Working with 3M Library Systems, ACRL is developing a strategic manual that includes "campaign messages and materials that focus on the value academic and research librarians and libraries play on campuses and within the community." (Orphan 2003) ACRL has also implemented an electronic discussion list - ACADEMICPR – to enable librarians to share their marketing and public relations ideas and best practices.

SURVEY PROCEDURE

In July 2003, 291 surveys were mailed to participating college and university libraries. Two e-mail reminders followed over a two-month period plus a third reminder with a copy of the survey. Some survey participants were telephoned as the deadline drew near. By October 31, 61% of the surveys had been returned. A request for specific documents, referenced in the completed surveys, was e-mailed to respondents in November 2003.

ANALYSIS OF SURVEY RESULTS

Is the process formal (planning activities and written policies in place) or informal (on-going, day-by-day activity)?

Although 52.5% believe marketing and public relations activities contribute to fulfilling the mission of the library (Question #1), only 4.1% had a formal marketing plan or a marketing strategy (Question # 9). Most personnel (68.9%) of those involved in marketing and public relations activities did not have this responsibility written into their job description (Question #15).

Respondents recognize marketing and public relations activity positively affects their library. Their approach to this function, however, lacks organization and structure indicated by the lack of a written policy. This lack of formal planning contradicts the best practices of successful businesses that follow a business plan to accomplish their goals and objectives. Marketing (which includes public relations) is a highly valued component of any business plan.

Library staff who generally performed this function in the library were not specifically responsible for this activity. This suggests that marketing and public relations receives a low priority. Respondents comments reflect a *do-it-as-I-can-get-to-it* approach.

Despite this, current job descriptions for librarians suggest a change in perception on the importance of marketing. Increasingly they include marketing and public relations responsibilities, as reflected it the following job titles: Communications Officer, Marketing Librarian, Outreach Librarian, Publicity Coordinator, Public Services Librarian.

According to the librarians surveyed, the four most important library marketing and public relations goals are as follows: stimulate use of the library's services (99.3%); stimulate use of the collections (91%); create greater perceived value of the library (88.4%); and influence institutional decision makers (71.1%) (Question #12).

Although respondents share the same goals and objectives (Question #12), librarians do not understand the marketing and public relations function or its benefits. All library activity - outreach or communication - is marketing. Public relations is an element of marketing. To accomplish the library's goal and objectives requires planning, user assessment and budgeting—all elements of a marketing plan which coordinates library activity. With a written action plan, librarians document their contribution to the institution and justify financial requirements, which, according to the current literature, increases funding as well as community support.

Two-thirds of the respondents (66.4%) indicated that they did not intend to develop a marketing plan or other written policy to coordinate marketing and public relations activities (Question #10). This position contradicts their belief that these activities (assessment, outreach, programming, etc.) are important (92.5 %) (Question #11). Again, this suggests that librarians do not understand the fundamental nature of marketing and public relations or its benefits.

With the increase in library marketing information and resources, librarians are becoming aware of the need for a written policy. Professional organizations (e.g., ALA, ACRL, SLA, IFLA), businesses (e.g., 3M Corporation, Lexis-Nexis, Gale Group, InfoToday), library schools and some libraries address the need for marketing and public relations practices by providing workshops, programs, classes, tool kits and Web sites to enable librarians to effectively perform this function.

What are the elements of this activity?

Marketing includes assessment and outreach, two professional tools used in libraries. This survey attempts to determine which marketing tools are most widely employed by librarians.

The librarians surveyed stated that the needs of their patrons are determined primarily by patron comments (81.9%). Web surveys (45.1%), e-mail surveys (19.2%), and outside consultants or services (22.5%) - such as LibQUAL+ - were also used. Individual interviews

(35.5%) constituted a significant means of needs assessment (Question #13). Individual interviews (35.5%) constituted a significant means of needs assessment (Question #13).

Needs assessment (a marketing tool) has been valued by librarians for decades. While electronic surveys have become popular, most libraries rely primarily on patron comments. Personal contact (public relations) with the library community - either at the reference desk or in the class room - is certainly a vital element of librarianship. As information management professionals, however, librarians should approach user needs assessment more systematically. By tracking, prioritizing and fulfilling user needs in a more structured manner librarians can better realize their goals and objectives while raising the credibility of the profession and their level of influence.

The distribution of brochures (81.3%) was the primary form of promoting (an element of a marketing plan) the library. Displays and exhibits are second on the list (80.2%) of important activities. Two-thirds of the survey participants depended on their library's Web site and e-mail communication (62.2%) as marketing and public relations tools. At least 55% of the respondents considered library programs an important activity (Question #24).

Brochures, displays and exhibits, and library programs are library staples for communication and interaction with the library community. The library's Web site provides anytime access to resources and services as providing brochures, and information about displays and exhibits, and programs. The institution's Web site and e-mail service also offers the library a convenient format for conducting a needs assessment.

Who is involved and what resources are available?

The role of any library director requires, as a matter of course, the establishment of effective communication with the library community (43.4%) (Question #16). Because of this role, the director generally initiates marketing activities. Often, this responsibility depletes the director's resources beyond the ability to effectively perform the marketing function.

But, the actual implementation of this function includes the director and librarians (55.4%) (Question #16). According to the literature, the recognized value of marketing to the library is creating a demand for librarians to expand their skills. The job titles and job descriptions currently reflect this trend in librarianship.

A plurality of respondents indicate only one or two library personnel (40.3%) are involved in marketing activities (Question #17), while the vast majority (81.8%) reported that only five hours-per-week or less of staff time are devoted to marketing (Question #18). This suggests again a fundamental lack of understanding about the scope and nature of marketing. Librarians do not realize that every activity used to fulfill the library's mission can incorporate facets of marketing: needs assessment, promotion, publicity. In fact, almost every aspect of librarianship has a marketing component, a component currently unrecognized.

According to the survey, most library personnel involved (74.4%) did not have marketing and public relations experience (Question #22) and 85% of the respondents reported that their library did not provide training (Question #23). Some participants do have an associate's degree in mass communications or business (29.2%) and a few had either a master's or bachelor's degree (Questions #19—#21).

Most library personnel who do marketing and public relations often find themselves performing this function by default. Those library personnel who have some knowledge of marketing or marketing experience tend to better understand its potential and use a more structured approach.

Most libraries had no monies specifically allocated for marketing and public relations activities (47.3%). Of those libraries reporting a marketing budget, only a very small percentage (5.7%) reported significant budgets of $1000 or more (Question #27). Outside funding was generally not available according to 83.9% of the respondents (Question #28).

Unfortunately, most library budgets do not include marketing and public relations expenses, except, for programs. This fact is a strong argument for a marketing plan which includes a budget, benchmarks and ongoing evaluation to track progress and make adjustments. Expenses for marketing in most libraries are limited to paper and printing which is deducted from the office supplies budget.

How effective is the effort?

The assessment of activity effectiveness, as identified in the formal/informal planning section of this analysis, included: patron comments, Web surveys, e-mail surveys and outside consultants or services (Questions #13 and #25).

Most respondents (86.7%) believe a planned and structured marketing program with written components would not benefit their library. But 46% of the survey respondents felt that their marketing and public relations activity benefits the library in the following ways (Question #30):

1) Heightened awareness of resources and services resulting in increased usage (46%)
2) Increased perceived value of the library resulting in funding (37.2%)
3) Improved perception of librarian value and credibility (4.9%)

With professional and business support as well as marketing resources becoming accessible, librarians are discovering the tools and the management skills to more effectively serve their community. Libraries that plan, track and evaluate their activity can document the extent and nature of their contributions to the institution. Facts, unlike perception, provide measures of the library's value and worth. The funding institution, like all businesses, is interested in their return on investment (ROI). The literature substantiates the claim that libraries do benefit financially from an organized and structured plan. Another reason for constructing a marketing plan is to improve the image of librarians. They become recognized as management professionals - not limited to free-service providers.

The most pressing deterrents to marketing and public relations activities include (Question #29): (Some respondents marked more than one answer)

1) Time constraints (62.8%)
2) Insufficient personnel (39.4%)
3) Lack of expertise (17.1%)
4) Inadequate funding (12.5%)

The literature indicates that unless librarians manage their time to prove the library's value and the librarian's worth to the institution, then librarians will be forced to find the time to defend themselves when budgets are cut or pay increases overlooked. Because more librarians now recognize the benefits of marketing and public relations practices, more libraries than ever before are hiring librarians with marketing and public relations experience and/or training.

CONCLUSION

- Although all librarians market their library's resources and services, they do not understand the elements of this function and/or its benefits.

- Few libraries have a written marketing plan or related document to guide library activity.

- Library directors generally initiate the activity, but librarians and support staff are involved in the implementation of activities.

- The library's annual budget does not usually include funding specifically for marketing. Expenses for brochures and other paper correspondence or promotion are drawn from the library's supply budget.

- Although most libraries agree that marketing and public relations activities benefit their library, they do not yet understand that a formalized approach would add focus and direction to their activities, with a more effective outcome that could be measured.

A marketing plan benefits the library like a business plan benefits an organization - a written policy that lists particular activities designed to achieve specific goals. A marketing plan includes the following elements: mission statement, identified target (patrons), an evaluation of the current situation, identified available resources, identified competition, promotional strategies with specific goals, and the monitor of activity to adjust strategy as needed.

The Association of College & Research Libraries (ACRL) *Standards for College Libraries 2000 Edition* prescribes to librarians a more progressive approach to marketing. The *Services* section states, "The library should establish, promote, maintain and evaluate a range of quality services that support the college's mission and goals." This standard serves as a strong indication of the philosophical support the profession is now giving marketing. This support is made stronger by the rich marketing resource materials, ranging from marketing tool-kits to marketing guides and an electronic discussion list, available from ALA through the @ your Library campaign.

Despite this some librarians resist and even resent the idea of marketing because they believe the value of their library to the community and their institution is self-evident. Although a gulf remains between the for-profit and nonprofit organizations as to the perceived value of marketing and public relations programs, the gap is closing.

If you want to achieve these goals: improve customer satisfaction; heighten the perceived value of the library, librarians and the profession; and insure the survival of your institution - then it is time to implement marketing and public relations practices.

SELECTED BIBLIOGRAPHY

Association of College & Research Libraries. "ACRL | Marketing @ Your Library Marketing." Available at: http://www.acrlissues /marketingyourlib /marketingyour.htm. Accessed 19 March 2004.

Association of College & Research Libraries, College Libraries Section Standards Committee. "Standards for College Libraries, 2000 Edition." Association of College & Research Libraries. Available at: http://www .ala.org/ala/acrl/acrlstandardscollegelibraries.htm. Accessed 19 March 2004.

Bates, Mary Ellen. "Free, Fee-Based and Value- Added Information Services." Ed. Donna Andersen. (April 2002) Factiva. Available at: http://www.factiva.com/collateral/files/ whitepaper_feevsfree_032002.pdf. Accessed 19 March 2004.

Cram, Laura. "The Marketing Audit: Baseline for Action." *Library Trends.* 43, (1995):326-349. In Expanded Academic [database online]. Accessed 19 March 2004. Available: Eckerd College Library.

Cutlip, Scott M. and Allen H. Center. *Effective Public Relations.* Englewood Cliffs, NJ: Prentice-Hall, 1994.

Ford, Vikki. "PR: The State of Public Relations in Academic Libraries." *College and Research Libraries* 46 (1985): 395-401.

Information Today. MLS Marketing Library Services. *(June 2002)* Information Today. Available at: http://www.infotoday.com/ mls/mls.htm. Accessed 19 March 2004.

Jarvis, Margo. "Anatomy of a Marketing Campaign." *Computers in Libraries* 18 (September 1998): 64-78. In Expanded Academic [database online]. Accessed 7 May 2002. Available: Eckerd College Library.

Kassel, Amelia. "Marketing: Realistic Tips for Planning and Implementation in Special Libraries; Market the Importance of Librarians, the Caretakers of Libraries Adapt to the Ever-Changing Forms of Knowledge." *Information Outlook* 6: 6-10. In Expanded Academic Index [database online]. Accessed 19 March 2004. Available: Eckerd College Library.

Kemp, Jane and Laura Witschi. *Displays And Exhibits in College Libraries. CLIP Notes #25.* Chicago: ACRL/ALA, 1997.

Kendall, Sandra and Susan Massarella. "Prescription for Successful Marketing." *Computers in Libraries* 21 (2001):28-34. In Expanded Academic [database online]. Accessed 19 March 2004. Available: Eckerd College Library.

King, Helen. "Stop!Here!" *The Australian Library Journal* 52 (2003): 90-92. In Expanded Academic [database online]. Accessed 19 March 2004. Available: Eckerd College Library.

Mahady, Tara. "Creating Community Through Your Communications." Campagne Associates. Available at: http://campagne.com/ community_print.html. Accessed 19 March 2004.

Morgan, Eric Lease. "Marketing Future Libraries." *Computers in Libraries 18 (1998): 50- 51.* In Expanded Academic [database online] Accessed 19 March 2004. Available: Eckerd College Library.

Orphan, Stephanie. "ACRL Marketing Efforts Expand." *American Libraries* 34 (2003): 10-12. In Library Literature and Information Science [database online] Accessed 19 March 2004. Available: Eckerd College Library.

Sass, Rivkah K. "Marketing the Worth of Your Library." *Library Journal* 127 (2002): 37-38. In Expanded Academic [database online].
Accessed 19 March 2004. Available: Eckerd College Library.

Smykla, Evelyn Oritz. "SPEC Kit: Marketing and Public Relations in ARL Libraries. SPEC Kit. 240; Summary". Association of Research Libraries, April 1999. Available at: http://www.arl.org/spec /240fly.html. Accessed 19 March 2004.

Special Libraries Association. "Public Relations, Marketing, Advocacy." Special Libraries Association. Available at: http://www.sla.org/ chapter/cwcn/wwest/v1n3/cavilb13.htm. Accessed March 19, 2004.

Wilson, Charlotte and Roger Strouse. "Marketing Tips for Information Professionals." 1 Feb 2002. In LexisNexis [database online]. tp:216.239.51.104 /search?q=cache:52uCoh3JSKAJ: www.lexisnexis.com/infopro/reference/pdf/MarketingTips.pdf+%2 2+wilson+and+strouse&hl=en&ieUTF-8. Accessed 19 March 2004. Available: Eckerd College Library.

CLIP Note SURVEY

Institution Information

1. Number of Full-Time Equivalent (FTE) students:
   Responses: 176

   Average: 3,020   Range: 13 - 25,000   Median: 2,400

2. Number of FTE faculty:
   Responses: 173

   Average: 184   Range: 4 - 1,000   Median: 80

3. Type of Institution
   Responses: 172

   Public: 53 (30.8%)   Private: 119 (69.1%)

Library Information

4. Number of FTE librarians
   176 Responses

   Average: 81   Range: 1 – 35   Median: 7

5. Number of FTE support staff:
   Responses: 172

   Average: 11   Range: 1 – 70   Median: 9

6. Number of student assistants (*fiscal year*):
   Responses: 159

   Average: 28   Range: 1 – 200   Median: 20

7. Annual Budget (*exclude salaries*):
   Responses: 159

   Average: $78,151
   Range: $33,433 - $5,200,200
   Median: $564,540

Marketing and Public Relations Planning

8. Who initiates marketing and public relations activities at your library?
    Responses: 176

a. Institution	25	(14.2%)
b. Director	153	(86.9%)
c. Librarian	90	(51.1%)
d. Staff	59	(33.5%)
e. Board member	3	(1.7%)
f. Friend of the library	11	(6.2%)
g. Student	2	(1.1%)
h. Other	2	(1.1%)

9. What *"written"* communications policy or procedures document does your library use to guide (establish, direct, coordinate) your library's marketing and public relations activity? (*mark all that apply*)
    Responses: 170

    a. Marketing Plan - a written plan of action that includes self-analysis, market research, establishing goals, designing strategies based on your research and evaluation   7   (4.1%)

    b. Mission Statement - a written declaration that describes thenature of your library, services offered, and community served   115   (67.6%)

    c. Public Relations Policy - a written communications plan, communications between the library and its users and potential users   16   (9.4%)

    d. Marketing Campaign - a series of activities designed to bring about a particular objective   22   (12.9%)

    e. Marketing Strategy - a statement describing how the library will obtain its objectives and an assessment   6   (3.5%)

f. Customer Service Policy – a library-user oriented
   philosophy that increases the value patrons receive
   when they use the library's resources and services 25   (14.7%)

g. No written document(s) in place   38   (22.3%)

h. Other   26   (15.2%)

   (Strategic Plan, Annual Report, Vision Statement,
   Institutional Communications Policy, Service
   Excellence Statement, University Public Relations
   Guidelines for Publications)

10. If you do not have a marketing plan or a public relations policy for
    your library, do you intend to develop one in the near future?
    Responses: 164

    a. Yes   53   (32.3%)
    b. No   109   (66.4%)
    c. Undecided   2   (1.2%)

11. How important do you believe marketing and public relations
    activities are to fulfilling the mission of your library?
    Responses: 175

    a. Very important   70   (40.0%)
    b. Important   92   (52.5%)
    c. Unimportant   8   (4.5%)
    d. Very unimportant   5   (2.8%)

12. What goal(s) does your library plan to achieve with its marketing and
    public relations activities? (*mark all that apply*)
    Responses: 156

    a. Stimulate use of library's services   155   (99.3%)
    b. Stimulate use of library's collections   142   (91.0%)
    c. Create greater perceived value of the library 138   (88.4%)
    d. Influence institutional decision makers   111   (71.1%)
    e. Increase funding   86   (55.1%)

f. Increase library program attendance	69	(42.2%)
g. Update image of librarians	51	(32.6%)
h. Attract non-institutional support of the library	47	(30.1%)
i. Raise the value of library and information science as a profession	36	(23.0%)
j. Other	3	(1.9%)

Marketing and Public Relations Implementation

13. What method(s) do you use to determine the needs of your library's patrons? (*mark all that apply*)
Responses: 177

a. Patron comments	145	(81.9%)
b. Web survey	80	(45.1%)
c. Focus group	74	(41.8%)
d. Individual interviews	63	(35.5%)
e. Other; internal surveys, external services	40	(22.5%)
f. Mail survey	35	(19.7%)
g. Not Applicable	3	(1.6%)
h. Telephone survey	2	(1.1%)
i. E-mail survey	34	(19.2%)

14. Who is responsible for the marketing and public relations activities at your library? (*choose one*)
Responses: 175

a. Director and librarian(s)	97	(55.4%)
b. Director	37	(21.1%)
c. Librarian(s) and support staff	17	(9.7%)

d. Other; Friends, PR Workgroup, Library Marketing
   Committee   15   (8.5%)

e. Librarian(s)   12   (6.8%)

f. Institution's public relations (communications)
    department   10   (5.7%)

g. Support staff   8   (4.5%)

15. Is the marketing and public relations responsibility included in the job
    description of the individual responsible for this function?
    Responses: 174

    a.   Yes   38   (21.8%)
    b.   No   120   (68.9%)
    c.   Not applicable 16   (9.1%)

16. What is the job title of the individual responsible for your library's
    marketing and public relations activity?
    Responses: 122

    a. Director   53   (43.4%)

    b. Other   47   (38.5%)

       (All library personnel, Public Relations Committee,
       Institutional Communications Department)

    c. Dean   8   (6.5%)

    d. Outreach Librarian   10   (8.1%)

    e. Public Services Librarian   4   (3.2%)

17. How many people (FTE staff and others) are typically involved in
    your library's marketing and public relations activities?
    Responses: 171

    a. 1-2   69   (40.3%)

    b. 3-4   42   (24.5%)

    c. More than 4   60   (35.0%)

18. Approximately how many hours-per-week are devoted to marketing and public relations activity? (choose one)

    Responses: 171

a. 5 or less hours	140	(81.8%)
b. 6-10 hours	25	(14.6%)
c. 11-15 hours	3	(1.7%)
d. More than 15 hours	3	(1.7%)

19. Do any of the personnel involved in your library's marketing and public relations activities have a master's degree in mass communications or business? (choose one)

    Responses: 174

a.	Yes	22	(12.6%)
b.	No	52	(87.3%)

20. Do any of the personnel involved in your library's marketing and public relations activities have a bachelor's degree in mass communications or business? (choose one)

    Responses: 173

a. Yes	31	(17.9%)
b. No	142	(82.0%)

21. Do any of the personnel involved in the library's marketing and public relations activities have an associate's degree in mass communications or business? (choose one)

    Responses: 171

a.	Yes	5	(29.2%)
b.	No	166	(97.0%)

22. Do any of the personnel involved in the marketing and public relations activities of your library have previous experience in marketing and public relations? (choose one)

    Responses: 174

a.	Yes	48	(27.5%)
b.	No	126	(72.4%)

23. Does the library provide or has the library provided any marketing and public relations training (workshops, online classes, etc.) for personnel involved in the library marketing and public relations process? (choose one)

Responses: 174

a.	Yes	26	(14.9%)
b.	No	148	(85.0%)

24. Which marketing and public relations strategies does the library use? (mark all that apply)

Responses: 172

a. Brochures	140	(81.3%)
b. Displays and exhibits	138	(80.2%)
c. Library Web site	113	(65.6%)
d. E-mail promotion	107	(62.2%)
e. Newsletters	96	(55.8%)
f. Library programs	94	(54.6%)
g. Networking	89	(51.7%)
h. Flyers	86	(50.0%)
i. Press releases	81	(47.0%)
j. Posters	81	(47.0%)
k. Advertisements	38	(22.0%)
l. Public service announcements	35	(20.3%)
m. Mail	35	(20.3%)
l. Other faculty training session, table tents, book marks, giveaways, public appearances, signage	27	(15.6 %)

25. How do you determine the effectiveness of your library's marketing and public relations activities? (*mark all that apply*)
Responses: 165

a. Patron comments	92	(55.7%)
b. Statistics	72	(43.6%)
c. Not Applicable	36	(21.8%)
d. Web survey	33	(20.0%)
e. Individual interviews	32	(19.3%)
f. Focus group	30	(18.1%)
g. Increased funding	26	(15.7%)
h. E-mail survey	15	(9.0%)
i. Mail survey	10	(6.0%)
j. Telephone survey	1	(0.6%)

26. Do you believe a planned and structured marketing and public relations program (a written plan of action, strategies, evaluation) would benefit your library? (*choose one*)
Response: 173

a.	Yes	23	(13.2%)
b.	No	150	(86.7%)

Please explain:

a. We don't do marketing

b. Believe services are self-evident, to feel we must 'sell it' makes us feel insulted, weary and discouraged.

c. Would be inappropriate for our campus environment

d. Small patron base so we rely on interaction

e. Defensiveness among some long time staff about PR, a resentment about feeling undervalued, underpaid and unappreciated

f. No one will take the lead; Not a traditional activity on a quiet campus

27. What is your Marketing and Public Relations Budget? (*mark all that apply*)
    Responses: 173

a. No monies allocated for marketing and public relations activities	82	(47.3%)
b. Less than $499.	42	(24.2%)
c. $500.and $999.	14	(8.0%)
d. $1,000. - $1,499.	8	(4.6%)
e. $1,500. - $1,999.	1	(0.5%)
f. More than $2000.	9	(5.2%)

28. Do any other *(non-institutional)* resource fund any of your library's marketing and public relations activities? (*choose one*)
    Responses: 174

a.	Yes	28	(16.0%)
b.	No	146	(83.9%)

29. What do you believe interferes with your library's marketing and public relations activities? (please rank, 1 being the greatest barrier)
    Responses:175

#1 Time constraints	110	(62.8%)
#2 Insufficient personnel	69	(39.4%)
#3 Lack of expertise	30	(17.1%)
#4 Inadequate funding	22	(12.5%)
#5 Other	15	(8.5%)
#6 Lack of interest	11	(6.2%)
#7 Personality conflicts	11	(6.2%)
#8 Organizational opposition	9	(5.1%)
#9 Differing expectations	8	(4.5%)

30. What to you believe is the one most valued effect of your marketing and public relations efforts?

   Responses: 102

   a. Heightened awareness of resources and services resulting in increased usage   47   (46.0%)

   b. Increased perceived value of library resulting in funding   38   (37.2%)

   c. Improved perception of librarian value and credibility   5   (4.9%)

   d. Other benefits include   12   (11.7%)

   * Better awareness of patron's needs

   * Raised awareness of censorship issues

   * Broader participation in collection development

   * Improvement in the quality of freshmen research

   * Increase in funding from donors

   * Increase in attendance at library programs and activities

   * Increased use of library by faculty for programs and displays

MARKETING AND PUBLIC RELATIONS DOCUMENTS

ANNUAL REPORT

ANNUAL REPORT

INFORMATION OUTREACH
Department/Unit

June 1, 2002 – May 31, 2003
(Period Covered)

June 2, 2003
(Date Submitted)

1. *What are the department/unit achievements for the past year? Indicate their relationship to college and department or unit mission and long-range goals.*

a. raised faculty awareness of our resources and services so that they, in turn, may promote them to (or even require) their students to use them in their coursework. This was accomplished primarily by holding demonstration/hands-on workshops for faculty generally and for individual departments, programs, and units (see Appendix A below)
b. explored the virtual reference marketplace to determine how we may enhance our own remote reference services using certain software and/or services that are available. This was accomplished by attending conferences, webcasts, and reviewing the professional literature.
c. organized the Library Lecture series aimed at highlighting PSU faculty research and their use of Library resources and services support their scholarship.

All three of these accomplishments support the unit mission to "provide expert information-finding and referral services free to our students, faculty, and staff, primarily, and to the general community as possible. We strive to identify and meet users' information needs and to create new services and programs that reflect the changing nature of the information environment. We also seek to guide users in developing their own finding and retrieval skills so that they may become more self-sufficient."

2. *How did department members participate in planning and assessment processes?*

Planning was done through unit meetings scheduled throughout the year. Our unit's assessment project (described in question #3 below) was planned by the unit members. carried out by our classified professional staff person and student assistants, and reviewed by the unit coordinator.

3. *How did students and other stakeholders (alumni, clients, community organizations, public or private) participate in planning, assessment, and other department/unit matters?*

They did not participate in any planning (but see question #7 below). Those who utilized the FLIER service (Feinberg Library's Individualized Extended Reference service) were sent an assessment survey though very few responses were received.

4. *What are the department/unit's major goals for next year, and how do you plan to achieve them? You may identify projects and you may also include timelines for completion, costs, and person(s) or group(s) responsible for each project.*

Our unit's long term operational goals are to 1) continue to raise awareness of our resources and services, and 2) to implement QuestionPoint, OCLC's virtual reference service, that are available. Tim Hartnett, unit coordinator, will assume primary responsibility for the latter. QuestionPoint training and implementation will occur from June-August 2003 so that the service will be fully available at the start of the Fall 2003 semester. The annual subscription cost for QuestionPoint is expected to be $2400-$3400.

5. *What are your long-term goals, and how do you plan to achieve them? You may identify projects and you may also include timelines for completion, costs, and person(s) or group(s) responsible for each project.*

My main unit goal for the year is to coordinate the successful implementation and promotion of QuestionPoint. This will be accomplished by immersing myself in the training and documentation and working closely with my colleagues at Feinberg (and possibly at other libraries should we choose to enter collaborative partnerships). Promotion will be delivered through the usual channels: all-campus emails, web bulletin board; posters; campus media ads; workshops; and library instruction (both LIB101 and course-related). Others promotion ideas will be welcomed and considered.

My non-unit goals include becoming re-involved with a learning community through LIB101 and becoming uninvolved with search committees! I hope to be part of a learning community for Fall 2004.

6. *What changes are you considering making in your programs or activities (i.e., developing, modifying, discontinuing)? Provide a rationale noting potential implications, both positive and negative.*

The unit is considering a reduction of service hours at the Reference Desk and/or staffing the desk at certain low-traffic times with non-librarians. The positive implication is that librarians hours may be better applied to other non-desk reference services such as QuestionPoint and FLIER. Secondly, it may serve to further invest non-librarian staff in the reference enterprise and facilitate their professional development. The negative implication is that the breadth and depth of desk service may be necessarily reduced during those targeted times.

We are also exploring wireless reference service options (using laptops, PDA's, and/or cell phones) to allow librarians at the reference desk or in their offices to roam in other areas of the building (book stacks, computer labs, etc.) while remaining connected to email, chat, and/or the web. While the implications are speculative at this tentative stage, we suspect that one positive implication is greater freedom to move to the physical location of a resource or user without breaking the continuity of service. Negatives include the librarians' learning curve, cumbersomeness of equipment, and dependence on wireless network and devices.

7. *If you wish to add any other information on your department/unit activities, plans, and accomplishments, please do so.*

In reference to question #3 above, the unit has not undertaken any needs assessments since it seems inherently obvious that we must continue to educate users about our resources and services and actively promote their use. Similarly, the national trend in virtual reference services and our own three-year experience using chat-based reference service compels use to enhance that service through an affordable, consortium-provided service (QuestionPoint).

Additional accomplishments include:

a. the addition of browser software for MS Word, MS Excel, and MS PowerPoint on the Electronic Search Center's workstations which enhances access to faculty course materials, government documents, and other internet resources

b. the creation of a reference desk question log in MS Excel format which enables us to undertake meaningful content analysis of the questions asked at the reference desk in person, by telephone, and by AOL Instant Messenger (IRef service).

APPENDIX A

Research in the 21st Century: Richer, Faster, and Better

Feinberg Library has steadily increased access to online digital resources, including full text journal databases, full text reference collections, multimedia files, electronic reserves, and current awareness services. Not only do they expand our Library's collections but they greatly facilitate the academic work of faculty and students alike. This session brings you up to date on our latest acquisitions and offers an opportunity for their guided, hands-on use. Learn how to enhance your course materials and engage students more deeply and easily in scholarship.

        Thu. Oct. 24 -- 3:00 PM (TIM)
        Thu. Nov. 7 -- 2:00 PM (DEBRA)
        Mon. Feb 17 -- 2:00 PM (TIM)
        Wed. Mar. 5 -- 1:00 PM (TIM)
        Tue. Apr. 1 -- 3:00 PM (TIM)
        Tue. Apr. 29 -- 2:00 PM (TIM)
        Mon. June 9 -- 1:00 PM (TIM)

Attendance: Approximately 60 people including VP'S, Deans, senior and junior faculty, staff and students.

APPENDIX B

INFORMATION OUTREACH UNIT ANNUAL REPORT FOR 2002-2003

Figure 1 below indicates steady decline in Reference Desk Activity from the previous year in all types of interactions except for Directional and Iref questions. While these are not unexpected trends given the overall decrease in library use, it is difficult to ascertain specific reason(s) for them. I sense that the Reference Desk is gradually becoming viewed more as a place for general informational, housekeeping service than for research assistance. This may provide some basis for reducing the number of service hours at the Reference Desk and/or staffing the desk at certain low-traffic times with non-librarians. The rise in IRef questions for the third straight year bodes well for our upcoming foray into the QuestionPoint Virtual Reference service.

Figure 1: REFERENCE & ESC STUDENT DESK ACTIVITY

Type of Interaction	2001-2002*	2002-2003	% CHANGE
Directional	899	1,042	15.9
Reference	9,695	8,209	-15.3
In-Depth	1,446	1,290	-10.8
IRef (Interactive)	369	402	8.9
FLIER Sessions	53	47	-11.3
Reference Email	53	42	-20.8
ESC Student Desk	22,950	18,560	-19.1
TOTALS	35,465	29,545	-16.7

The 2001-2002 data errors have been corrected since last year's annual report and the figures in this column are the revised totals.

ATTACHMENT C

ASSESSMENT RECORD FOR ADMINISTRATIVE OR EDUCATIONAL SUPPORT DEPARTMENTS/UNITS

INFORMATION OUTREACH UNIT
(Name of Administrative or Educational Support Department/Unit)

June 1, 2002 – May 31, 2003   *June 2, 2003*
(Assessment Period Covered)   (Date Submitted)

Department/Unit Mission Statement: The mission of the Information Outreach unit is to provide expert information-finding and referral services free to our students, faculty, and staff, primarily. and to the general community as possible. We strive to identify and meet users' information needs and to create new services and programs that reflect the changing nature of the information environment. We also seek to guide users in developing their own finding and retrieval skills so that they may become more self-sufficient.

Title of Program/Project:

FLIER service (Feinberg Library's Individualized Extended Reference service)

Submitted by: *Tim Hartnett*   Title: *Information Outreach Coordinator*

Form A

ASSESSMENT REPORT FOR

FLIER service (Feinberg Library's Individualized Extended Reference service)
(Program or Project Title)

June 1, 2002 – May 31, 2003
(Assessment Period Covered)

June 2, 2003
(Date Submitted)

Note: One Form C should be completed for each intended outcome listed on Form B. The intended outcome should be restated in the space below and the intended outcome number entered in the blank spaces.

Intended Outcome: An effective FLIER service provides highly personalized and comprehensive research assistance to develop a discernible search strategy to meet users' information needs beyond what is possible through the standard, walk-in, first-come first-serve assistance available at the Reference Desk.

First Means of Evaluation for Outcome Identified Above

a. Method of Evaluation and Criteria for Success: FLIER service users will be sent an email survey within one week after their FLIER session. Those users who do not respond within a week will be telephoned by a designated and trained Student Assistant and asked to complete the survey or respond directly over the telephone to the survey questions. Data will be compiled by the unit Classified Professional and shared with the unit members for review and analysis.

Criteria for success are

- 90% of all FLIER appointments will be scheduled at a time convenient for the user
- In 100% of all FLIER sessions the librarian understand and explore users' information needs
- In 80% of all FLIER sessions will result in a discernible search strategy to meet users' information needs
- In 80% of all FLIER sessions will result in the identification of a wide array of useful sources of information to meet their needs

Note: Benchmark figures set by unit based on its sense of reasonable expectations

a. Summary of Evidence Collected: 36 surveys were distributed and only 8 responses were received. These responses were overall quite positive but the sample is too small to yield any conclusive results. We intend to continue to offer the FLIER service.

Information Outreach Unit's 2003-2004 Initiatives

1. Implement QuestionPoint, OCLC's virtual reference service.

The main unit goal for the year is to coordinate the successful implementation and promotion of QuestionPoint. This will be accomplished by immersing ourselves in the training and documentation and working closely with colleagues at Feinberg (and possibly at other libraries should we choose to enter collaborative partnerships). Addressing issues of librarians' reference workload is central to the success of this implementation. Promotion of QuestionPoint will be delivered through the usual channels: all-campus emails, web bulletin board; posters; campus media ads; workshops; and library instruction (both LIB101 and course-related). Other promotion ideas will be welcomed and considered.

Status: In process
Timeline: Training in July-August -- go live by 8/25/03.
Funding: $2280 annual subscription fee plus minimal training travel and promotional expenses ($200-$300)
Lead Unit: Information Outreach

2. Improve outreach efforts to faculty to increase awareness and use of our resources and services.

Activities may include email alerts, liaison visits to departments, generic or custom hands-on workshops, subject guides for the Feinberg web page, etc.

Status: In process
Timeline: Ongoing
Funding: Minimal promotional expenses ($100-$200)
Lead Unit: Information Outreach

3. Reinforce frequent, intellectual use of Feinberg Library's resources through the Library Lecture Series and the Library Film Series.

The Library Lecture series highlights PSU faculty research and their use of library resources and services support their scholarship. It may be possible to invite other non-campus scholars to speak about their research and how libraries and librarians have played a pivotal role. The Library Film series is co-sponsored by Campus Life, which underwrites the film rental cost. The Library promotes the films and their topics by preparing concise bibliographies of relevant library and web resources to be posted on our Library web page.

Status: In process
Timeline: Ongoing
Funding: Minimal promotional expenses ($100-$200)
Lead Unit: Information Outreach

ASSESSMENT REPORT FOR

FLIER service (Feinberg Library's Individualized Extended Reference service)
(Program or Project Title)

June 1, 2002 – May 31, 2003   *June 2, 2003*
(Assessment Period Covered)   (Date Submitted)

Note: Please complete one Form B for each program or project listed on Form A.

Expanded Statement of Institutional Purpose Linkage

> PSU Mission Statement Reference: Our FLIER service identifies and meets users'
> information needs and guides them in developing their own finding and retrieval skills so
> that they may become more self-sufficient. Thus FLIER "prepares a diverse student
> population for a wide range of professional careers by providing undergraduates with a
> strong foundation in the liberal arts, graduate students with advanced professional
> preparation, and all students with a commitment to academic excellence, ethical values,
> lifelong learning, and responsible citizenship within a global community" [PSU Mission
> Statement]

> Division Mission Statement Reference: to provide leadership and support in the
> areas of information resources including technology, access, exchange,
> programming, and information and computer literacy. Library and Information
> Services directly informs, educates, and supports all aspects of the educational
> mission of Plattsburgh State University. All programs and policies of the
> Division strive to be responsive to the needs of students, faculty, staff, and the
> community.

> PSU College-wide Student Outcomes Supported (if relevant): All supported to some
> degree, but especially numbers 1-6.

Intended Outcomes for this Program or Project (include student outcomes if relevant):

1. An effective FLIER service provides highly personalized and comprehensive research
assistance to develop a discernible search strategy to meet users' information needs beyond what
is possible through the standard, walk-in, first-come first-serve assistance available at the
Reference Desk.

Form B

a. Use of Results to Improve Unit Services: See above

Second Means of Evaluation for Outcome Identified Above:

___.b. Method of Evaluation and Criteria for Success: None developed

___.b. Summary of Evidence Collected:

___.b. Use of Results to Improve Unit Services:

Form C

EXHIBITS AND EVENTS PLANS

Planning Events and Creating Displays
(REQUIRED READING)

<u>Announcements</u>

It is almost always appropriate (even necessary) to announce the display or event in one or more places:

♦ Campus *Communicator* (daily)
Send e-mail to announce@goshen.edu by 7:00 am the day you want the announcement to run; let them know how many days to run it. If you want a "fresh" announcement in the "New Announcements" section each day, you'll need to submit a new announcement each day (preferably worded differently or with a different angle each time).

♦ *Faculty-Staff Bulletin*, a/k/a FSB (weekly on Fridays)
Send e-mail to announce@goshen.edu by 9:00 am on Thursday for publication in the next day's FSB. Remember that this is a newsletter for faculty and staff only, so you may want to re-word announcements, give a bit more detail, or otherwise alter your style and/or content

♦ *Record* (weekly)
This is a student paper, written by students and for students. It's not always easy to get an interview or a piece published about a particular initiative, especially if it doesn't seem really interesting to students. (This doesn't mean it's not important – only that it may lack a perceived newsworthiness for this particular medium.) Contact the student editor if you have ideas. One other caveat: A *Record* editor or reporter may come calling some time when you're not trying to get attention. They may ask for you to write a "Perspectives" (op-ed) piece, or they may want to interview you about something that you don't think is such a big deal. If this happens, please contact Lisa GC before granting an interview or giving statements about library activities, policies, etc. (You just never know how things may be interpreted or presented in a different context than originally intended.)

♦ On-campus posters [more info to come]

♦ Off-campus venues [more info to come]

e-mail: announce@goshen.edu

Planning Events and Displays
(REQUIRED READING)

<u>Supplies & tools</u>

- We have a supply of colored paper, sign holders, tabletop display stands, slatwall accessories (for the 3-part display board to the right of the circ desk), adhesives and other supplies that may be used for creating displays. All of these materials are stored together in a cabinet in the large library work room. Feel free to use what you need and put back leftover stuff that might be reusable when you're done with a project.

- The library color printer is also available for creating banners and signs associated with displays. This is the "library color laser" or "libr-2" printer option in most of your applications. If you can't find this printer option, please ask for help installing the proper drivers on your PC.

- Microsoft Word and Microsoft Publisher are both useful for creating display materials. If you haven't used Publisher and are planning to create a display, you should take some time to explore and try it out.

- If you need special supplies, resources or assistance in creating a display or planning for an event, contact LH or LGC to start.

<u>Guidelines for choice of fonts, colors and type sizes</u>

- The "official" fonts of GC are Garamond and Helvetica ("AGaramond" is also used). While we aren't strictly required to use only these fonts for temporary displays, I would like anyone who is doing informational text and lettering for a display to stick to fonts that are fairly straightforward and plain, as opposed to *fancy script-type* fonts, **gimmicky** or *goofy* fonts, **faux-old style**, or other *hard-to-read* fonts. Major headings can be more *Stylized*, but keep in mind that the more information you have to get across, the plainer the text should be. Style should <u>enhance</u> content rather than obscure or compete with it.

- Try to avoid ALL CAPS <u>except</u> when you're doing a HEADING of some sort. ALL CAPS FOR LOTS OF TEXT IS ALSO HARD TO READ.

- Don't go overboard with *italics*, shadowing, or other **<u>special effects</u>**.

Planning Events and Displays
(REQUIRED READING)

♦ Make sure there's enough   white space   between important pieces of information. This applies to both text and graphics.

♦ Don't use light colors that are   .

♦ Keep content brief and catchy, with a mix of graphic elements and text. Don't cram pages and pages of prose into a display.

♦ Text size should be big. **12 point is never big enough for important information, and 14 point is usually not big enough either.** Obviously, you will have some limitations presented by the format of the materials you're working with (a screen print from a web page, for instance). However, when possible, **aim for at least 18 point as the very smallest type size in the display** (a bibliography, for instance). **Headings should always be larger.**

♦ Heading text should be **bold**. Some fonts don't lend themselves to bolding because there's not a lot of difference between the thickness of the regular font versus its **bold version**. (Unfortunately, Garamond and AGaramond are two such fonts.)

♦ When in doubt, do a draft first and run it by LGC and/or others on staff.

/lgc
10-1-2003

**Library Displays
2002-03**

When	Theme	Elements to include	Who	Where
2002-09	Wendell Berry's visit to campus	- Date, place, time, etc. - Books in our library by Berry	Kathy K.	3-part board: LEFT panel
2002-09	9/11	- Terrorism & peace themes - John Roth's recent book - David Cortright's recent interviews - Books in the library	Ryan	Library Lobby (front & center)
2002-09	Welcome (and Welcome back)	- "Watch this space" message - Library events	Lisa	3-part board: RIGHT panel
2002-10	Alumni Weekend	- Photo of Harold & Wilma Good, GC alums? - Books by "famous" GC alums?	Kathy P.	3-part board: LEFT panel
2002-10	Faculty Promotions	- Books selected for the library by recently-promoted faculty members	Sally Jo & Susan	Library Lobby (front & center)
2002-10	Thomas Frank, 10/18 convo speaker	- Convo date & brief biographical info on Frank - Several pertinent quotes - Two books by Frank (we'll need to purchase them ASAP)	Lisa	3-part board: LEFT panel
2002-10	Mennonite Writing Conference (Oct. 24-27)	- Basic info about the conference (when, where, highlights, etc.) - Brief bios of some of the featured speakers - Books in the library written by some of the featured speakers	Jessica	Library Lobby (front & center)

**Library Display Schedule
2002-03**

2

When	Theme	Elements to include	Who	Where
2002-10	SA Yoder Lecture & Yoder Public Affairs speakers	- Info on the events (two convos and an evening lecture) - Books by the speakers (Patrick Friesen, Sandra Birdsell, Robert Orr)	Kathy K.	3-part board: LEFT panel
2003-03	Gordon Kaufman's visit to campus	- Books and quotes by/about Kaufman - Schedule of lectures/events	Lisa	3-part board: LEFT & RIGHT panels
2003-05	CALL Grant	- What it is - Library materials purchased with grant funds	Susan & Sally Jo	Library Lobby (front & center)
2003-05	Graduating student library workers	- Bios & photos of seniors who work in the library	Kathy P. & Laura	3-part board: LEFT & RIGHT panels

FUNDRAISING PROPOSAL

REQUEST FOR DIVERSITY COMMITTEE FUNDING

The Diversity Committee's goal is to increase understanding of diversity at UMF in the curriculum and co-curriculum. Our general education requirements include a comparative cultural perspectives portion which states that students will "be aware of their own cultural heritage. beliefs. values. and behaviors. and we expect this awareness will encourage students to respect the freedom of others to have beliefs. values. and behaviors different from their own."

According to the UMF Diversity Plan. diversity "includes such important and intersecting dimensions of human identity as race. ethnicity. national origin. religion. gender. sexual orientation. class. age. and ability."

The Diversity Committee has a modest amount of money to grant to faculty. staff. and students who want to launch projects that will further its goals. which are 1) to educate ourselves about diversity: 2) to improve the campus culture: and 3) to work with our local region to appreciate differences.

Without limiting your creativity. we can suggest that some things likely to be funded might be presentations. workshops. materials. and professional development/conference attendance.

How can we be so ambitious with a modest amount of money? Because we want diversity to be embedded in our classrooms. student events. and other activities. Therefore. we want you to consider other funding sources (such as departments and student organizations). **Preference will be given to proposals jointly funded by one or more other entity.**

1. __**PRISM Committee, Mantor Library**_____
    Name of person(s) and/or organization(s) applying

2. __**116 South Street, Farmington, ME 04938**_____

    __**x7224**____**shellyd@maine.edu**_____
    Address, phone, e-mail

3. Describe your project:
"One Book, One Campus"
    The goal of this project is to have everyone on the UMF campus read *The Chosen*, a novel by the late Chaim Potok. Prior to the "One Book, One Campus" events we will make copies of the book available at the library, and direct those who wish to purchase a copy of the book to appropriate sources. A Web site of information and links to online resources will be created. During the "One Book, One Campus" week, we will:
    *   **facilitate discussion groups so that the UMF community can come together to discuss the novel;**
    *   **hold a word search contest;**
    *   **put up displays of resources and information;**
    *   **host one or more speakers from within the UMF community and from outside;**
    *   **show the film adaptation of the novel, as well as other relevant films. We hope to include a documentary if a suitable one can be located.**

4.   Anticipated date of project: (These projects may occur any time before 5/15/2002.)

We announced the title for this year's "One Book, One Campus" on October 11 in order to give faculty time to think about how they might implement this program in their Spring semester courses. During winter break, we will arrange for events and speakers, and create the Web page and promotional materials. We hope to begin publicizing the schedule of events at the beginning of Spring semester. Some activities (such as discussion groups) would take place in February and March, and the program will culminate with a week of films and speakers in late March or early April.

5.   Who else will be carrying out the work of this project?
The Mantor Library PRISM committee will be planning the project. We will continue to encourage staff, faculty, and students to offer suggestions and to participate in the scheduling and carrying out the events.

6.   We will make grants from $50 to $1000. How much do you need? How will you spend it? (Please give us a detailed budget.)
Known costs:
>   **Showing the film version of *The Chosen* and another film (possibly *Fiddler on the Roof* or *Yentl*)$400.00**
>   **Renting a documentary, for a public viewing – $50.00**
>   **Publicity (printing posters, fliers, bookmarks, etc.) – $50.00**
>   **Incentives to attend events (food, prizes) – $150.00**
Unknown Costs:
>   **Speakers – We are looking into locating speakers for this program who could give presentations and facilitate discussions on the themes of the novel. We have identified a faculty member who has agreed to do a presentation for us, and we're exploring possible speakers from off-campus as well. In order to keep costs down, we are looking within the state, and at the farthest, New England.**
>   **Books – We would like to have a supply of copies of *The Chosen* so people will be able to read the novel without having to purchase it.**

Our known costs total $650 at this point. We estimate the total cost of the program will not exceed $850, so we are requesting approximately $750 from the Diversity Committee.

7.   List anyone else who is helping to fund it. How much have they committed?
The Mantor Library has committed $100.00 to this project. The library's PRISM committee members have committed their time and effort to planning and implementing this program. PRISM members will be creating the Web page, designing displays and promotional materials, organizing activities, and facilitating discussions.

8.   Who do you intend to reach?
We intend to reach the entire UMF campus as well as interested community members.

9. How will this work further the goals of diversity education?

The book, *The Chosen* is the story of two Jewish boys growing up in Brooklyn, NY during World War II. Reuven comes from an Orthodox Jewish family; his father is an intellectual who supports the Zionist movement. Danny is the eldest son of an Hasidic rebbe, or rabbi; according to Hasidic tradition, he will be the congregation's next rebbe. Against the background of the war in Europe, and the emerging awareness of the Nazis' persecution of European Jews, *The Chosen* offers a look at the richness of the Jewish faith and the traditions within that faith - something our everyday experience in rural Maine might not provide. In doing this, the novel dispels misconceptions of Judaism as a single, simple religion. Too often, a religious designation conjures up a one-dimensional image or stereotype - Catholics have large families, Jews are doctors or lawyers, Muslims hate Americans. It is our hope that reading and talking about *The Chosen* will increase our awareness of differences within a religious tradition and that readers will apply this understanding to other faiths as well, so that all traditions are recognized as complex and multidimensional. The novel also deals with universal issues of faith, loyalty, friendship, and the expectations others have of us, which makes it easier, perhaps, for us to understand and identify with the characters.

As in last year's "One Book, One Campus" program, our goal is to get everyone at UMF to read the same book at the same time, and to use a shared reading experience as an opportunity to interact with one another while increasing our awareness of and appreciation for people whose backgrounds and traditions may not be the same as ours.

Please submit to Valerie Huebner in intra-campus mail. Questions can be addressed to her at ext. 7258 or huebner@maine.edu

ROLLING DEADLINE

MARKETING CAMPAIGN

Library Administration and Management Association

a division of the American Library Association
50 East Huron Street. Chicago, Illinois 60611

312-280-5038
Fax: 312-280-5033
Toll Free: 800-545-2433
http://www.ala.org/lama

January 25, 2003

Nancy Magnuson
Julia Rogers Library
Goucher College
1021 Dulaney Valley Road
Baltimore, MD 21204-2794

Dear Nancy:

Congratulations! Your library has been selected as a winner in the 2003 John Cotton Dana Library Public Relations Award Contest.

60 entries were submitted for this prestigious annual award, which has been presented continuously since 1946. The award recognizes outstanding achievement in the promotion of library services. Winning entries such as yours set the standard for excellence in library public relations.

This international contest has been jointly sponsored for fifty-four years by the American Library Association's Library Administration and Management Association and The H. W. Wilson Company. A panel of judges from the LAMA Public Relations Section spent 3 days of deliberation selecting the winners.

The 2003 awards were announced on Saturday, January 25, at a special press conference at the ALA Midwinter Meeting in Philadelphia, Pennsylvania. Your award will be presented at a ceremony hosted by The H. W. Wilson Company during the ALA Annual Conference in Toronto, Canada. An invitation to the event will be forthcoming.

We realize that successful public relations programs rely on a team effort. Therefore, we hope that you and the one or two colleagues most responsible for this winning entry will be able to participate in the awards ceremony. You will be contacted concerning the name of the person or persons who will be accepting your library's award at the ceremony.

Winning entries will be displayed at the JCD Exhibit booth and the LAMA PRS Swap & Shop Program in Toronto. We invite you and your staff to join us at the "Best of Show" Swap & Shop program, on Sunday, June 21, and we suggest that you bring extra promotional items to share. Following the conference, the ALA Library and Resource Center will retain your winning entry for two years to send to interested libraries via interlibrary loan.

The entire committee joins me in applauding your winning entry. We look forward to seeing you in Toronto.

Sincerely,

Tim Wadham
Chair, LAMA PRS John Cotton Dana
Library Public Relations Award Committee

TW/akm

December 23, 2002

John Cotton Dana
Library Public Relations Award Committee
American Library Association/LAMA
50 E. Huron St.
Chicago, IL 60611

Dear Committee Members:

I am pleased and proud to submit our entry for the John Cotton Dana Library Public Relations Award, *Twenty-Five Years of Jane Austen:* A Milestone Celebration, on behalf of the Julia Rogers Library staff and the entire Goucher College community. The campaign described in the application album was truly a collaborative effort to bring world-wide attention to the gem that is the Burke Austen Collection.

A campaign that seeks to highlight a rare and fragile special collection must balance preservation with public relations. We can invite only a select few for intimate access to the materials, and for others, mediated experiences must suffice. Our goals were:

- to call greater attention to the collection among literary scholars and to prompt new and serious scholarly use of material;
- to extend Goucher College's reputation to a wider community of those who conduct scholarly research;
- to instill within the many segments of the Goucher community a sense of pride in the collection and its positive contribution to intellectual life on campus; and
- to celebrate the devoted efforts and elegant style of Alberta and Henry Burke in the pursuit of "everything Jane" and further fulfill their dream that others would enjoy the collection as they had.

At each of the four steps of the process, assessment, planning, implementation and evaluation, we matched goals and intended audiences with appropriate strategies.

We successfully linked Jane Austen and Goucher College in the minds of scholars and bibliophiles on an international level and made our own community aware of its unique good fortune. Perhaps the most exciting notion is that *Twenty-Five Years of Jane Austen* will continue to reap benefits to the college for many years to come. Thank you for your consideration.

Sincerely,

Nancy Magnuson
College Librarian

Twenty-Five Years of Jane Austen: A Milestone Celebration

INTRODUCTION

Upon her death in 1975, Goucher College alumna Alberta Hirshheimer Burke, '28, bequeathed her beloved Jane Austen Collection to the Julia Rogers Library at Goucher. The collection, containing nearly 1,000 volumes and roughly 33 linear feet of additional materials, was created over a period of 40 years. It includes many rare first and foreign language editions, as well as important books related to fashion, gardening and home furnishings of the Regency period. Mrs. Burke and her husband Henry traveled extensively in pursuit of Austen material and in 1936, Mrs. Burke began pasting articles, playbills and poems – nearly 2,800 clippings – in a series of ten composition notebooks. She called this very personal journal of appreciation "References and Allusions to Jane Austen." Goucher College is proud to be the home of the Burke Collection of Jane Austen, one of the great masters of the English novel. Few small undergraduate institutions are so fortunate.

NEEDS ASSESSMENT

The primary impetus for the *Twenty-Five Years of Jane Austen* public relations campaign was the recognition by the Julia Rogers Library staff, under the direction of college librarian Nancy Magnuson, that the milestone offered a unique opportunity to call attention to its most prestigious collection, to numerous significant events since the gift was received and to the rare qualities of Alberta Hirshheimer and Henry Burke.

A number of circumstances inspired the planning. For example, during the 1990's, the work of Jane Austen enjoyed a revival of sorts, due in part to the success of several motion pictures based on her novels. As a result, the staff realized that today's college students had greater exposure to Austen characters and dialogue and were poised to take a more scholarly interest in her work. Further, technology has made the impossible possible. Today, any interested person with Internet access can become acquainted with far-off collections that, in years past, would have remained undiscovered. Fragile and rare materials are well served by digital display, while online catalogs allow researchers to identify holdings of distant libraries.

At Goucher, the library underwent a renovation that added a reading room equal to the collection it hosts. The room provides a safe environment for the materials and an inviting one for scholars. And last, but certainly not of least importance, at the 25-year mark, the faculty of Goucher College includes teachers who highlight the work of Jane Austen in popular English department courses. Those faculty members also have cemented ties to the community of Austen appreciators known as Janeites. Professor Laurie Kaplan serves as the editor of *Persuasions*, a scholarly print journal, and *Persuasions On-Line*, an electronic version, both published by Jane Austen Society of North America. Assistant Professor Carol Pippen is the editor of JASNA*News*, a newsletter published by the same group. The library staff realized that the twenty-fifth anniversary of the Burke gift was an opportune time to bring together these many resources and collaborate with other college departments to shine a light on the collection.

PLANNING

The challenge of calling attention to a collection of fragile material is to balance "trumpeting" and "preserving." It is not possible - nor appropriate - to put the collection at risk for the sake of publicity. The *Twenty-Five Years of Jane Austen* campaign was designed to maintain that balance.

Campaign goals were established: 1) to call greater attention to the collection among literary scholars and to prompt new and serious scholarly use of material, 2) to extend Goucher College's reputation to a wider community of those who conduct scholarly research, 3) to instill within the many segments of the Goucher community a sense of pride in the collection and its positive contribution to intellectual life on campus, and 4) to celebrate the devoted efforts and elegant style of Alberta and Henry Burke in the pursuit of "everything Jane" and further fulfill their dream that others would enjoy the collection as they had.

Target groups were identified as: Goucher College students, faculty and staff; Goucher alumnae/i and donors; scholars and students at other institutions; the Baltimore community; and the community of Janeites, through the international Jane Austen Societies.

Strategies were devised:
- Creating the Burke Austen Scholar-in-Residence Program

To encourage scholarly use of the collection, the staff devised a residence program consisting of financial support, opportunity for public recognition and wide outreach for potential users. Seeding the work of scholars and letting them "spread" the word about the depth of the collection is a very personal, but effective, form of public relations. The competitive process of soliciting applications allowed a review team to evaluate requests with an eye towards the best opportunity to highlight the collection itself. Publicizing the competition placed Goucher on a national stage.

The Burke Endowment Fund made it possible to offer a $1,000 stipend and up to $1,500 in travel and lodging expenses to scholars, which was particularly important given the general decline in travel and grant funds available to university faculty. In addition to conducting research with the Austen materials, the scholar was invited to deliver a public lecture and meet with faculty and students during a one-week stay.

- Publishing Printed Material

A retrospective booklet was designed to serve as a keepsake reminder and "calling card" for the campaign. The library staff sought outside expertise as appropriate. Professor Laurie Kaplan and Nancy Magnuson composed the text and the Office of Communications staff developed a "look" that suited the subject. The publication was a creative and financial collaboration. Collateral materials were prepared for numerous events.

- Integrating Traditional College Events

Two significant college events highlighted the anniversary. The Development Office featured *Twenty Five Years of Jane Austen* at one of its Annual Fund Receptions and at Commencement 2001, an honorary degree was presented to Joan Austen-Leigh, a descendant of Jane Austen and one of the founders of JASNA.

- Redesigning the Jane Austen Website: URL: http://www.goucher.edu/library/austen_home.htm

During the *Twenty-Five Years of Jane Austen* campaign, librarian Barbara Simons, long-time champion of the collection, and Linda Fowble of the instructional technology department co-authored a Goucher College Strategic Initiative Grant to purchase a camera and light stand. Their goal was to digitally capture Alberta Burke's notebooks with the least amount of risk to the material. On-line availability is key to capturing the attention of the younger generation and enabling those at greater distances to explore the collection.

- Issuing Press Releases

The media was notified about the Scholar-in-Residence program, the selection of Professor Mary Favret as the first scholar, the public lecture given by Professor Favret and the unveiling of the Alberta Burke's Notebooks website.

IMPLEMENTATION

November 2000: A press release was issued announcing the silver anniversary of the collection and the establishment of the biennial Scholar-in-Residence grant.

December 2000: The anniversary booklet was published and mailed, with customized cover letters, to over 3,500 people and nearly 30 organizations. The last page included a formal announcement of the newly created Scholar-in-Residence program. A timeless document, it is still distributed at events and is available to visitors to the rare book room. It is also available in PDF format on the Jane Austen website.

January – April 2001:

Advertisements calling for applications to the Scholar-in-Residence program were published in *The Chronicle of Higher Education* and on several university websites. Laurie Kaplan highlighted the program in the Editor's Note of *Persuasions,* Vol. 23, and Carol Pippen featured it in the JASNA*News,* Spring 2001 edition. Six inquiries were made leading to four applications from faculty members of prestigious institutions in the United States and Canada. Supporting recommendations were received from scholars at the National Humanities Center, Princeton University, McGill University, City University of New York and Wheelock College.

February 2001: At a gathering held to honor the 40th anniversary of JASNA in Maryland, Nancy Magnuson presented a history of the Burkes as collectors and shared copies of their correspondence about the collection.

March 2001:
As a part of the Annual Fund Campaign, a gathering to support The John Franklin and Mary Fisher Goucher Society was held on March 23 at the Julia Rogers Library. Over 40 people attended the evening program, "Cocktails and Conversation Featuring 25 Years of the Jane Austen Collection." Event planners specially invited Goucher alumnae/i and local friends of the college who might have a particular interest in Austen. Hosts and speakers for the event were selected on the same basis. The Burke Jane Austen Collection was a unique draw; over half of the guests had never attended a fundraising event.

The library display cases contained valuable first editions of Austen's novels while nearby computers displayed Goucher's Jane Austen website. The anniversary booklet was placed on display with specially designed Austen return envelopes for donations. Together, the three Annual Fund events raised $24,000 in new or increased gifts.

May 2001: At Commencement, Joan Austen-Leigh, hospitalized in Vancouver, received an honorary doctorate from Goucher via speakerphone. Professor Laurie Kaplan's presentation speech, heard by over 800 persons attending Commencement, highlighted the contributions of Dr. Austen-Leigh and the significance of the Burke Austen Collection.

June 2001: A special exhibit from the collection was prepared for the annual conference of the Society of Dance History Scholars, held at Goucher.

September 2001: Mary Favret, Assistant Professor of English from Indiana University, was selected as the first Scholar-in-Residence.

September - October 2001: A team of Goucher students designed and organized the "Alberta Burke's Notebooks" website. The notebooks were photographed by an additional team of Goucher students - a time-consuming, physically demanding process - while the design team added interactive elements to the site.

November 2001 –February 2002: Planning for Professor Favret's visit began. Invitations to the public lecture were sent to the Board of Trustees, the Alumnae & Alumni of Goucher board of directors, members of the Baltimore Academic Libraries Consortium, the Maryland Independent Colleges & Universities Association, the Baltimore and Washington, D.C. JASNA chapters and the Baltimore Bibliophiles. A press release was issued detailing the itinerary.

March 2002: The Scholar-in-Residence program was held March 4 - 8. Professor Favret spent 20 hours alone with the collection; her very presence and interest in the collection as someone _not_ associated with Goucher validated its significance for members of the campus community. During the week, she taught Professor Kaplan's English Literature survey class, mesmerizing nearly 40 students on the connections between Austen's _Emma_ and the poetry of William Wordsworth, receiving an ovation at the end of the 8:30 a.m. class. She was the guest of honor at an afternoon tea, attended by faculty, staff and students who had an opportunity to interact with her informally. At the end of the week, she delivered a public lecture, "Jane Austen and Everyday War." The audience of over 80 was comprised of students, faculty, alumnae and alumni, members of Friends of the Library and faculty from other schools including Towson University, Morgan State University and the University of Maryland at College Park. The lecture was featured in the _Goucher Quarterly_, which is mailed to all alumnae/i, and in _FOCUS_, the newsletter of the Friends of the Library.

May – July 2002: The "Alberta Burke's Notebooks" website went through a final phase of testing.

November 2002: A press release announced the launch of Alberta Burke's notebooks on-line.

EVALUATION
Twenty-Five Years of Jane Austen was designed to have both short- and long-term effects. In particular, the over-arching goal of making the Burke Austen Collection a "destination for scholars" is expected to be a gradual rather than an immediate reality. In the short term, the campaign reached its target audiences with great success. Complimentary letters about the booklet were received from around the world, including one from Dr. Austen-Leigh who remarked on the "many treasures and discoveries to be found in the booklet together with nostalgia for a

vanished age." The Jane Austen Society (England) and the Jane Austen Society of Australia requested additional copies, and JASNA distributed 550 copies at its Annual General Meeting. Professor Favret was impressed with what she referred to as a "treasure trove" and was "spurred to new ideas for projects on Austen and Austen lovers." Students, staff, faculty and alumnae/i became involved in the collaborative effort. All events were well attended and received, drawing first-time visitors to the campus.

Publicity reached a wide and international audience, with coverage in:

- *Persuasions*, Vol. 23, circulation 4,000
- Spring 2001, Summer 2001 and Spring 2002 JASNA*News*, circulation 4,000
- June 2001 JASA News, The Jane Austen Society of Australia online newsletter at http://members.ozemail.com.au/~jasa1/newsju01.htm
- Nation On-line, a Bangladeshi news source, February 2001 at http://www.nation-online.com/200102/05/n1020509.htm
- The April 2001 edition of *Matrix*, a magazine aimed at college administrators with a circulation of 42,000+

Even before the *Twenty Five Years of Jane Austen* campaign was over, it had already inspired several additional events further raising awareness of the collection:

November 2001: Nancy Magnuson was invited to give a presentation on the Burke Austen Collection at Washington College in Chestertown, Md., sponsored by the Friends of the Clifton M. Miller Library.
January 2002: The Baltimore Bibliophiles held an evening of "Jane Austen Charades" in honor of the Burke Austen Collection.
April 2002: Lisa Richmond, the Library Director at St. John's College in Annapolis, Md. brought a group of students to visit the collection.
July 2002: The local chapter of the Jane Austen Society held its summer meeting at the Julia Rogers Library. The group of 28 enjoyed a classic English tea and then visited the Burke Austen Collection in the reading room as well as "virtually" from the Multi-media Center. The preview of "Alberta Burke's Notebooks" web site was particularly popular.
January 2003: Nancy Magnuson will make a presentation about the collection to the 200 member Baltimore Lecture Group, an 80 year old organization, based at the Baltimore Hebrew University.
April 2003: A group of Janeites from Virginia scheduled a visit to Goucher and the Burke Collection, inspired by a preview of the Notebooks web site during an Austen seminar taught by Carol Pippen at the Smithsonian Institute.

The goal of establishing the collection as a destination for scholars is within sight. Professor Favret serves as an informal ambassador of the Burke Austen Collection and continues to develop research material gathered during her residency. As she put it, "it may be years before I exhaust what I've gleaned." She gave two lectures in England in November of 2002 in which she used and formally acknowledged materials found in the Burke Austen Collection. She is scheduled to present a paper next summer at a conference in Chawton, England titled "Women's writing in Britain 1660-1830." She is planning two publications for next spring. Because new scholarship builds on what has come before, seeding individual scholars is comparable to dropping stones in a pond – multiple circles widening their reach.

Thousands of individuals, both in the United States and abroad, have been exposed to this unique collection and the important contribution of the Alberta and Henry Burke. Requests for appointments are increasing. The library staff expects that the second Scholar-in-Residence program scheduled for the spring of 2004 will be received with great interest and involve a more intense application process. Subsequent residencies will not be linked to anniversary milestones therefore different strategies will be developed to maintain the higher profile achieved by this campaign. For those who cannot take advantage of the Scholar-in-Residence program or visit the collection in person, "Alberta Burke's Notebooks" on-line offer an intimate look at her handiwork and devotion to Jane Austen.

John Cotton Dana Award Application 2003
Julia Rogers Library
Twenty Five Years of Jane Austen
<u>**Book Layout**</u>

<u>Left</u> Page #	Contents	<u>Right</u> Page#	Contents
Inside Cover	Alberta H.Burke bookplate	1	blank leaf
2	4/76 Library News Clipping	3	Text & scanned pictures of 1st editions and notebooks
4	BLANK	5	**Needs Assessment Divider**
6	Glossy Picture of Reading Room	7	Text & scanned pictures of visitors to collection and Persuasions cover
8	BLANK	9	**Planning Divider**
10	Booklet Layout Draft	11	Full Page of Text
12	BLANK	13	**Implementation Divider**
14	BLANK	15	Text & November 2000 Press Release
16	Booklet Cover Letter	17	Text & Booklet in Pocket
18	Booklet Spread	19	Booklet Spread
20	Scholar-in-Residence Ads	21	Text & JASNA News in Pocket
22	BLANK	23	Text & February 2001 JASNA Meeting Handout in Pocket
24	Color Pictures & donation envelope	25	Text & 2001 Development Meeting Invitation
26	Editor's Note Persuasion Vol. 23	27	Text & May 2001 Inkwell in Pocket
28	Dance Scholars Website	29	Text & June 2001 Dance Bibliography in Pocket
30	BLANK	31	Text & September 2001 Press Release
32	BLANK	33	Text & Scanned pictures of photography process and notebook page
34	Invitation to Favret Lecture	35	Text & February 2002 Press Release
36	Goucher Quarterly story	37	Text & b/w picture of Mary Favret in reading room
38	Color pictures from lecture	39	Focus Issue on Lecture in pocket
40	Notebooks website picture	41	Text & Notebooks website picture
42	BLANK	43	Text & November 2002 Press Release
44	BLANK	45	**Evaluation Divider**
46	BLANK	47	Text & Joan Austen-Leigh's letter

48	Letter from Brian Southam	49	Letter from Susannah Fullerton
50	Letter from Mary Favret	51	Letter, cont.
52	Nation Online website	53	Matrix magazine article
54	Nancy Magnuson at Washington College poster	55	Text & Invitation to Washington College event, Baltimore Bibliophiles Charades bookmark
56	July 2002 JASNA tea pictures	57	Text on later events & Thank you note
58	BLANK	59	Text on long-term goals of campaign; quote from Alberta H. Burke
60	BLANK	Back Cover	BLANK

Malissa Ruffner
December 2002

MARKETING PLANS

Scott Community College Library

Marketing Plan

2003-2005

SCC Library Marketing Plan
January 2003–December 2005
Table of Contents

SCC Library Mission Statement......................... Page 1

SCC Library Vision Statement........................... Page 1

Purpose of Marketing Plan............................. Page 1

Relationship of the SCC Library
Marketing Plan to EICC Planning Documents........... Page 1

Target Groups... Page 1

Needs of the Targeted Groups.......................... Page 2

Library Strengths and Challenges....................... Page 2

Future Trends... Page 3

Goals and Objectives.................................. Page 4

Timeline.. Page 8

Credits... Page 11

SCC Library
Marketing Plan
January 2003-December 2005

SCC Library Mission Statement

The mission of the Scott Community College Library is to serve the students, faculty, and staff of SCC by providing access to informational materials and services and by teaching patrons how to use these resources.

The library will reflect an active commitment to excellence, to life long learning, and to cooperation with the wider community.

SCC Vision Statement

Responding to a changing lifelong learning environment, the SCC Library is committed to providing timely, easily accessible, user-friendly informational materials and services.

Purpose of the Marketing Plan

The purpose of the Marketing Plan is to develop a logical, organized, manageable plan that incorporates input from library customers and markets library services, programs, and resources to SCC patrons.

Relationship of the SCC Library Marketing Plan to EICC Planning Documents

The Library Plan, in the Marketing section, page 8, focuses on the need for a Marketing Plan and enumerates several methods the library currently uses to market its services to patrons. This plan is written to become a part of the SCC Library Plan and will provide goals, objectives, and a timeline to further the SCC Library's commitment to inform patrons about library resources and to teach patrons how to access and use these resources. The SCC Vision Statement and the SCC Library Mission Statement point to these goals.

EICCD Key Performance Indicator, number 3, states: "The EICCD develops and maintains quality curricula and services which anticipate and support local, national, and global needs". The Marketing Plan, through its goals, objectives and timeline of promotional materials and activities, will be in keeping with this standard.

Target Groups

The targeted groups for the promotional materials and activities of the library are the faculty of Scott Community College, adjunct and full time, staff of Scott Community College and students of Scott Community College.

SCC Library
Marketing Plan
January 2003-December 2005

Needs of the Targeted Groups

The needs of these two groups and the library's strengths and weaknesses were determined from a survey done in the spring semester 2002. These surveys were distributed to measure student and faculty satisfaction with library materials and services. The Library plan, in Assessment and Outcomes Assessment, points to the document "The Eastern Iowa Community College District Assessment System: A District wide System to Improve and Support Student Leaning". The SCC Library Mission statement is two-fold, to provide access to information and services and to teach patrons how to use these resources. In order to meet with its mission, the library conducts surveys to measure patron skills in using its resources. Copies of both surveys are included.

Students
- Become more knowledgeable about library services and resources.
- Special needs students need knowledge of library services, such as the Optelec Clear View.
- To learn research skills:
  a. To determine what resources to use for their projects.
  b. Database search skills.
  c. To design a research plan.
  d. How to cite sources for bibliography.
  e. Critical and original thinking in the research and writing process.
- To learn how to access, use and evaluate information in a variety of formats.

Faculty
- Knowledge of library resources-both electronic and print and how these resources can help students complete assignments.
- Knowledge of library services and how the services can support them individually and how they can support their students.
- Develop cooperative partnerships and benefits of the partnerships to them individually and to the students.

Library's Strengths and Challenges
Strengths
- Knowledgeable, resourceful, and service-minded staff.
- Service minded library committee; members represent a range of educational departments.

SCC Library
Marketing Plan
January 2003-December 2005

Library's Strengths continued

- Electronic databases-covers wide range of subjects suited to student needs on a community college campus.
- Collection development to support curriculum.
- Information Literacy services.
- Other library services, such as interlibrary loan, on-line holds, QuadLINC phone renewals, fax, cassette copy services, individual instruction, and copies of telecourses on video.
- Other materials we provide to answer student queries concerning other services at EICCD and information concerning community services for students.

Challenges

- Remodel library facilities to meet the changing needs of customers.
- Space.
- Certain portions of our collection need development.
- Uncomfortable seating and lighting.
- Need of more computers for student research.
- Need of place to hold instruction sessions (student disturbance) and need for sessions to be "hands on."
- Communication with faculty needs to be increased for collection development, bibliographic instruction, reference, and reserve services.

Future Trends

Library materials will increase in electronic databases and electronic journals. The Internet will continue as a change agent in the use of library print and subscription database resources. The trend toward electronic development of library materials will make library resources readily available from home or other off campus computers. Promotional materials and activities should create a desire or need to go to the library for instruction and educational support. One challenge is marketing our resources to online users through the SCC Library's web page. Another challenge is to market library services to patrons on campus.

SCC Library
Marketing Plan
January 2003-December 2005

Goal 1: Market the SCC Library to students.

Objective (Activity)	Start date	Completion Date	Assessment Method
Increase student use of the library for research by 2% per year.	May 2003 May 2004 May 2005	Fall 2005	A combination of database statistics, reference statistics, and interlibrary loan statistics.
Design and distribute bookmarks about database research. Distribute bookmarks to Student Life Center, Kahl Virtual Library, and MTC.	Spring 2003 Fall 2003	Fall 2003	Number of bookmarks handed out.
Promote Turn off TV week in April.	Spring 2003 Spring 2004 Spring 2005	Spring 2005	Contest entries, number of flyers picked up.
National Library Week	Spring 2003 Spring 2004 Spring 2005	Spring 2005	Number of flyers or other materials picked up.
Border's days to promote library awareness and reading in general.	Spring 2003	Spring 2003	Money received.
Library card sign up week.	Fall 2003 Fall 2004 Fall 2005	Fall 2005	Number of applications. Number of entries for gift certificate.
Conduct library use surveys during the spring semester.	Spring 2003 Spring 2004 Spring 2005	Spring 2005	Survey statistics.
Conduct library open house for students	Spring 2004 Spring 2005	Spring 2005	Drawing entries.

SCC Library
Marketing Plan
January 2003–December 2005

Goal 2: Market the SCC Library to faculty.

Objective(Activity)	Start date	Completion date	Assessment method
Develop a library marketing advisory group. The purpose of this group is to provide input to Library Staff on marketing tools and activities for the library and to help develop assessment tools. This group will consist of several members of the SCC Library Committee, 2 faculty members, 2 students, and an SCC staff member. The group will meet twice a year, in person or via email.	January 2003	January 2003	Number of suggestions from committee.
Appoint members to an advisory group.	January 2003	February 2003	Number of persons nominated and number of accepted positions.
Initial meeting with advisory group members	March 2003	April 2003	Attendance record and minutes of meeting.
Meet with advisory group members once a semester	November 2003 April 2004 November 2004 April 2005 December 2005	December 2005	Attendance records

SCC Library
Marketing Plan
January 2003–December 2005

Goal 2: Market the library to faculty continued

Objective (Activity)	Start date	Completion date	Assessment method
Maintain a list of full time and adjunct faculty from SCC, Kahl, and MTC.	Spring 2003 Fall 2003 Spring 2004 Fall 2004 Spring 2005 Fall 2005	Fall 2005	Is list up to date?
Faculty and staff reception during Banned Books week	Fall 2004 Fall 2005	Fall 2005	Drawing entries.
Design and distribute newsletters for faculty once at the beginning of each semester. Distribution via mailbox and Intranet.	Spring 2003 Fall 2003 Spring 2004 Fall 2004 Spring 2005 Fall 2005	Fall 2005	Completion of project.
Distribute survey concerning newsletter.	Fall 2003 Fall 2004 Fall 2005	Fall 2005	Survey response.
Prepare resource lists for specific SCC departments.	English: Fall 2003 Nursing/Allied Health: Spring 2004 Biology: Fall 2004 Childcare: Spring 2005	Fall 2003 Spring 2004 Fall 2004 Spring 2005	Completion of project.

SCC Library
Marketing Plan
January 2003–December 2005

Goal 3: Market the SCC Library to staff.

Objective	Start date	Completion date	Assessment method
Maintain a list of staff from SCC, Kahl, and MTC.	Spring 2003 Fall 2003 Spring 2004 Fall 2004 Spring 2005 Fall 2005	Fall 2005	Is list up to date?
Design and distribute flyers about library services of interest to staff: Quad-LINC system, library cards, interlibrary loan access accounts, and digital cameras.	Spring 2003 Spring 2004 Spring 2005	Spring 2005	Staff applications for library cards and Access accounts, checkout of digital cameras, staff interlibrary loans.
Place announcements on the Intranet and Internet to staff about the library as informational support on wellness materials, fiction books for pleasure reading, materials to increase knowledge on computer technology and software applications.	Spring 2003 Fall 2003 Spring 2004 Fall 2004 Spring 2005 Fall 2005	Fall 2005	Completion of tasks.

SCC Library Marketing Plan
January 2003-December 2005
Timeline

Spring Semester 2003

January — Design and distribute newsletter to faculty via mailboxes and Intranet. (Goal 2)

January — Develop and appoint members of a library marketing advisory group. (Goal 2)

February — Distribute survey concerning newsletter to faculty. Distribution should be by mailbox. (Goal 2)

February — Design and distribute flyers about library services of interest to staff. (Goal 3)

March — Design and distribute bookmarks about database research. (Goal 1)

March — Initial meeting with advisory group members. (Goal 2)

April — Promote "Turn Off TV Week." (Goal 1)

April — Promote National Library week. (Goal 1)

April — Place announcement on Intranet and Internet about library materials of interest to staff. (Goal 3)

April — Promote Border's Days to increase library awareness and reading. (Goal 1)

May — Create, distribute and tabulate library use surveys. (Goal 1)

May — Compile database statistics, reference statistics, and interlibrary loan statistics. (Goal 1)

Other activities to be completed spring 2003

- Maintain a list of full time and adjunct faculty from SCC, Kahl, and MTC. (Goal 2)
- Maintain a list of staff from SCC, Kahl, and MTC. (Goal 3)

Fall Semester 2003

August — Design and distribute bookmarks about database research. (Goal 2)

August — Design and distribute newsletter to faculty via mailboxes and Intranet. (Goal 2)

August — Announcement on Intranet and Internet about library materials of interest to staff. (Goal 3)

September — Distribute survey concerning newsletter to faculty. Distribution should be by mailbox. (Goal 2)

September — Library Card Sign-up week. (Goal 1)

September — Hold faculty and staff reception during Banned Books Week. (Goal 2)

October — Prepare resource list for English Department. (Goal 2)

November — Meet with library marketing advisory group. (Goal 2)

Other activities to be completed fall 2003

- Maintain a list of full time and adjunct faculty from SCC, Kahl, and MTC. (Goal 2)
- Maintain a list of staff from SCC, Kahl, and MTC. (Goal 3)

SCC Library Marketing Plan
January 2003-December 2005
Timeline

Spring Semester 2004

January	Design and distribute newsletter to faculty via mailboxes and Intranet. (Goal 2)
February	Distribute survey concerning newsletter to faculty. Distribution should be by mailbox. (Goal 2)
February	Conduct library open house for students. (Goal 1)
February	Design and distribute flyers about library services of interest to staff. (Goal 3)
March	Prepare resource list for Nursing/Allied Health department (Goal 2)
April	Promote "Turn Off TV Week." (Goal 1)
April	Promote National Library week. (Goal 1)
April	Meet with advisory group members. (Goal 2)
April	Place announcement on Intranet and Internet about library materials of interest to staff. (Goal 3)
May	Create, distribute and tabulate library use surveys. (Goal 1)
May	Compile database statistics, reference statistics, and interlibrary loan statistics. (Goal 1)

Other activities to be completed spring 2004

- Maintain a list of full time and adjunct faculty from SCC, Kahl, and MTC. (Goal 2)
- Maintain a list of staff from SCC, Kahl, and MTC. (Goal 3)

Fall Semester 2004

August	Design and distribute newsletter to faculty via mailboxes and Intranet. (Goal 2)
August	Announcement on Intranet and Internet about library materials of interest to staff. (Goal 3)
September	Distribute survey concerning newsletter to faculty. Distribution should be by mailbox. (Goal 2)
September	Library Card Sign-up week. (Goal 1)
September	Hold faculty and staff reception during Banned Books Week. (Goal 2)
October	Prepare resource list for Biology Department. (Goal 2)
November	Meet with advisory group members once a semester. (Goal 2)

Other activities to be completed fall 2004

- Maintain a list of full time and adjunct faculty from SCC, Kahl, and MTC. (Goal 2)
- Maintain a list of staff from SCC, Kahl, and MTC. (Goal 3)

SCC Library Marketing Plan
January 2003–December 2005
Timeline

Spring Semester 2005

January	Design and distribute newsletter to faculty via mailboxes and Intranet. (Goal 2)
February	Conduct library open house for students. (Goal 1)
February	Distribute survey concerning newsletter to faculty. Distribution should be by mailbox. (Goal 2)
February	Design and distribute flyers about library services of interest to staff. (Goal 3)
March	Prepare resource list for Childcare Department. (Goal 2)
April	Promote "Turn Off TV Week." (Goal 1)
April	Promote National Library week. (Goal 1)
April	Meet with advisory group members. (Goal 2)
April	Place announcement on Intranet and Internet about library materials of interest to staff. (Goal 3)
May	Create, distribute and tabulate library use surveys. (Goal 1)
May	Compile database statistics, reference statistics, and interlibrary loan statistics. (Goal 1)

Other activities to be completed spring 2005

- Maintain a list of full time and adjunct faculty from SCC, Kahl, and MTC. (Goal 2)
- Maintain a list of staff from SCC, Kahl, and MTC. (Goal 3)

Fall Semester 2005

August	Design and distribute newsletter to faculty via mailboxes and Intranet. (Goal 2)
August	Announcement on Intranet and Internet about library materials of interest to staff. (Goal 3)
September	Library Card Sign-up week. (Goal 1)
September	Distribute survey concerning newsletter to faculty. Distribution should be by mailbox. (Goal 2)
September	Hold faculty and staff reception during Banned Books Week. (Goal 2)
September	Distribute survey concerning newsletter to faculty. Distribution should be by mailbox. (Goal 2)
December	Meet with advisory group members once a semester. (Goal 2)

Other activities to be completed fall 2005

- Maintain a list of full time and adjunct faculty from SCC. Kahl, and MTC. (Goal 2)
- Maintain a list of staff from SCC, Kahl, and MTC. (Goal 3)

Scott Community College Library
Marketing Plan
Spring 2003-Fall 2005
Credits
Scott Community College Library
500 Belmont Road
Bettendorf, Iowa 52722
(563) 441-4150   email: scclibrary@eicc.edu
URL: http://www.eicc.org/library/index.html

<u>**Library Committee**</u>

Mark Aronson
Kirk Barkdoll, ex officio
Carol Caldwell
Vicki Gray
Barb Hixon
Jeannine Ingelson
Herb Meyer
Linda Nelson
Mark Newman
John Turner
Yvette Work

<u>**Library Staff**</u>

Jane Campagna
Linda Nelson
Carol Brade
Joyce Haack
Ann Imhoff
Bernice Meredith

For further information contact:

Jane Campagna   or   Linda Nelson
Associate Dean of Learning Resources   Library Assistant I
563-441-4152   563-441-4151
jcampagna@eicc.edu   lnelson@eicc.edu

We value and appreciate all those who have provided their thoughts and expertise in the development of this plan.

Marketing Plan
To Increase the Visibility
Of the
Mildred F. Sawyer Library

Submitted to Robert E. Dugan, Library Director

By Kristin N. Djorup, Senior Reference Librarian

November 14, 2000

Table of Contents

Mission and Purpose   Page 1

Characteristics and Trends of the Operating Environment   Pages 2-3

Overview of Customers and Products   Pages 3-5

Strategies and Actions   Pages 5-9

Issues for Further Consideration   Pages 9-13

Timetables for Strategies   Appendices A-D

Cited References   Appendix E

Mission and Purpose

The Sawyer Library is one of seven academic resource centers that facilitates the University's mission to "provide academic services for people of various levels of preparation and ability" (see Catalog). According to the library's own mission statement, the library "contributes to the overall mission of the University by making available, and providing access to, informational resources and qualified staff to support the teaching, learning and research needs of CAS and SSOM students, faculty and staff." (see Mission) The Sawyer Library would like to increase its visibility, in order to attract more students and faculty to the library. By increasing visibility, the library hopes to draw attention to the fact that "informational resources" encompass a wide range and depth of content that is multidisciplinary and substantive in nature. It is a primary goal that people begin to appreciate the range and complexity of the resources available in support of their subject areas, and that they take advantage of these resources as they progress through their educational experiences. It is only by using these resources that the University community will appreciate their value. The library would like usage to be as robust as possible, in order to help with prospective planning and budgeting. By getting an accurate reading of this usage, the library will be better able to plan for the future.

Characteristics and Trends of the Operating Environment

The need for on-site and 24/7 off-site access to materials, the depth and breadth of university programs, and the emphasis on multicultural and varied points of view, require that resources be broad and multidisciplinary. Fortuitously, with the trend toward electronic publishing, the publishing world actually encourages the multidisciplinary dimension of this resource provision. Increasingly, periodical articles, reports, and reference and trade books are being published in electronic form; the medium itself allows for large amounts of material to be available from the same vendor through the use of standardized search methods. Databases of indexing and often the full-text of periodical articles use sophisticated search structures that have incorporated issues such as copyright and quality control into their designs.

Furthermore, the publishers are going through constant mergers and acquisitions, with a large number of publications consolidating under the same vendor interface. This trend impacts pricing. For example, a vendor offers two versions of a database product; one is a "global" version with 2000 full-text titles, the other is an "elite" version with 1500 full-text titles. The only real difference is the number of titles, so that the one with 2000 titles costs more than the one with 1500 titles. Also, publishers base their pricing on the number of full-time equivalent students. Libraries respond in kind, by joining consortia of like institutions, in order to take advantage of discounted pricing by larger groups of full-time equivalent students. The library benefits, as the resource becomes affordable, because of the volume discount. Also, the arrangement promotes goodwill among other members of the consortium, as additional numbers of full-time equivalent students increase the possible discount for everyone.

Overview of Customers and Products

The library's customer base is primarily Suffolk undergraduate and graduate students, faculty, staff, and to a lesser extent, students and faculty from Fenway Library Consortium schools. Students use course materials on Reserve, study space, Reference materials, periodicals, general books, and electronic databases. While research stations provide free printing and downloading capabilities for use in accessing the electronic databases, students take advantage of off-site access to these databases, as well. Database access from remote campus programs is through off-site access, only. However, of the 5,032 students who were enrolled in CAS and SSOM who were enrolled in Suffolk programs in 1999, 4,749 or 94% of them were actually enrolled on the Boston campus. (see FAQ) Many of these students actually live off campus, so it is convenient for them to be able to do their research from off-site. Furthermore, students are becoming increasingly computer-savvy, and many of them use the World Wide Web routinely for email, web surfing, stock quotes, news, and other information. These students are often unaware of the value of licensed library arrangements for electronic databases that provide primary and secondary periodical literature, with the added benefits of paid copyright arrangements, quality control over the printed text, and enhanced search techniques and strategies for accessing the material. An implicit goal of this marketing plan is to make the student more aware of the value of these electronic databases over and above the other information that the student accesses through the web.

Although the overall student headcount for the Boston campus was 4,479 students in 1999, the FTE for the University itself was 3,952 students. Roughly 79% (3114) of the FTE population is undergraduate. Although these students divide slightly under two to one into CAS over SSOM (see FAQ), students in the management programs must also enroll in courses that are taught within CAS departments, in order to fulfill their degree requirements. This means that library resources for the SSOM students alone, must be multidisciplinary enough to support a wide range of student projects. Furthermore, 838 of the 3,952 FTE students are graduate students, with CAS programs accounting for a little over one third (230 of 608). The majority of the graduate students study in SSOM programs. Library resources must not only be multidisciplinary, but they must also be rich enough to support the depth and breadth of the range of master's degrees offered through CAS and SSOM and the recently accredited Ph.D. in Clinical Psychology.

In addition to the resources available to the students, the Faculty has access to Interlibrary Loan and Document Delivery options, where the Sawyer Library borrows monographs or acquires periodical articles from other libraries or through an off-site vendor. This has implications for the operating budget, as the library must project an allocation for borrowing - rather than purchasing - a number of monographs, and the copyright and handling fees of articles related to faculty and Ph.D. student research.

These funds represent money that is spent over and above the money spent on Reserve textbooks and readings, circulating books, and printed and electronic Reference and Periodical resources.

Therefore, although the library's customer base is primarily undergraduate students and to a lesser extent graduate students and faculty, the needs of these populations are diverse and multidisciplinary. These needs require a wide range of both printed and electronic resources, with some instruction in the use of the various interfaces that are required in order to access the information that is contained within the resources. The library tries to make a range of resources available to the students, faculty and other people who use the resources, with a range of services designed to help facilitate the use of the collections.

Strategies and Actions

This area provides a description of four key strategic areas that are designed to increase library visibility. Each of these areas addresses a separate approach to promoting the library's resources and services. Several activities designed at promoting the library are suggested for each area. The strategy areas to be considered by this plan are: Promotion, Positioning, Learning, and Research. The following sections discuss each of these areas, in turn. See the Appendices for Timetables for the various activities.

Strategy Area 1: Promotion

This area addresses tangible ways to increase library visibility. The emphasis with these activities is to advertise the library, to create associations between the name "Mildred F. Sawyer Library" and the physical location of the library in the Sawyer building. This section suggests different activities to promote the library. The attached Appendix A shows a timetable that provides the number and frequency of each activity or event.

1. Place ads in the **Suffolk Journal**

2. Make available pens with the library name and URL

3. Hold a No Fine Day

4. Conduct an Open House in the Spring (during National Library Week):

    Hold demos of resources, refreshments, drawing for prizes (pizza, gift certificate to Borders, tee shirt with "Mildred F. Sawyer Library" and Suffolk seal on it.) By holding it during National Library Week, we draw attention to the concept of "Library."

5. Hang a TV near the stairwell with library "ads" on it, like the teletext system used in the Law Center

Strategy Area 2: Positioning

These activities have focus on location and presence. The library has a physical front door on the lobby level of the Sawyer building and a web presence on the University web server. Students and faculty may enter either entrance in order to gain access to a myriad of information resources and services. We welcome suggestions from visitors should anyone wish to contact us. The attached Appendix B provides a timetable for implementing activities.

1. Move the library front sign from the bricks on the side to the front door over the library. If the best way to draw attention to a library is to build a new building, the least costly alternative might be to move the sign!

2. Set up a suggestion box in the library near the windows.

3. Place a suggestion button on the library web page.

4. Design and print mouse pads with the library name (This is not the computer lab!)

5. Devise and send a survey to each individual administrators (all deans, associate deans, etc.) in both CAS and SSOM to see how they perceive the library as a useful resource within the missions of the individual schools.

6. Revisit the library's mission statement to consider whether or not "informational resources" is a strong enough term to convey the wide range and depth of resources available at the academic center known as the Sawyer Library. (We know what we mean, but does the user community appreciate

that there is actually a lot of content and substance included under the

umbrella of "informational resources?")

Strategy Area 3: Learning

This strategy focuses on students. These activities emphasize the ways that

library resources enhance the learning process. The library offers a range of electronic

databases that provide indexing and full-text of reports and articles, as well as books and

other materials. We provide training sessions in the use of the resources, and the staff

assists people with search strategies and information gathering. Feedback is welcome, so

that we can take a reading of whether or not the library clientele finds the resources to be

accessible. See the attached Appendix C for a timetable.

1. Conduct library orientation sessions at beginning of the Fall semester.

2. Offer drop-in library orientation sessions.

3. Convene a student library committee - Advertise the committee through

   Student Activities and on library web site.

4. Distribute an evaluation survey at end of each academic year - Ask what

   resources are especially helpful.

5. Hold subject sessions on resources for specific disciplines - Advertise these

   sessions through academic departments.

6. Distribute an "Expectations" survey at the beginning of the Fall semester to

   find out what incoming students expect from the library.

Strategy Area 4: Research

This area emphasizes Faculty Research. Although the faculty is comfortable with research tools in chosen disciplines, people are often not aware of new electronic resources and methods of finding material. These activities emphasize the different avenues for presenting information to faculty on new acquisitions. See Appendix D for a timetable for different activities.

1. Write and distribute memos to Faculty describing new databases

2. Develop newsletters to Faculty and students - Post them on the Web and print paper copies for distribution

3. Conduct orientation sessions for faculty on specific databases

4. Develop "New book (and video) lists" - Post them on the web and distribute them in print

5. Conduct a survey of faculty to determine what library resources they feel are useful to students when doing course related assignments within the discipline taught by the faculty member

Issues For Further Consideration

Measurement

In order to assess whether or not usage of library resources has increased, it is necessary to have a baseline figure from which to begin to measure. Some possible sources for baseline measurements are:

- IPED statistics to determine how many people ask questions or borrow materials

- Library Entrance Counter to determine how many people have entered the front door

- Proxy server statistics to determine database usage from off-site

- Web page counters to determine how many people look at the main library web page, the list of selected web sites, and the database menu

- Qualitative surveys from which to extrapolate levels of perceived satisfaction (such as an "Expectations" survey to find out what incoming students expect from the library, followed by an "Evaluation" survey at the end of the year, to find out if the library has met expectations)

Future Residency Requirements and Their Impact on the Library

When more residential students live on campus, will they need a central library as a focal point, or will they do most of their research from their rooms? Will they need a 24 hour reading room/computer lab as there is at Dean College? What will be the impact of these new configurations on

- Spatial arrangements

- Library collections

- Technology

- Accommodations for part-time students

<u>Satellite Campuses</u>

This marketing plan addresses our Boston campus, primarily; this approach is appropriate, as 94% of our Fall 2000 FTE enrollment is on the Boston campus. (see Enrollment) How aggressively should we advertise our resources at our satellite campuses?

- Merrimack

  As the old saying goes, "if it ain't broke, don't fix it!" Over the most recent academic year (99/00), no Suffolk student enrolled in the Merrimack program asked any questions or made any complaints related to the Sawyer Library of the librarians at the McQuade Library at Merrimack College! If we have very few students at the site, it may be premature to do any active marketing. As of Fall 2000, we have 42.9 FTE students enrolled in Suffolk programs at Merrimack.

- CCCC

  Students at the Cape campus are bound geographically, unless they wish to travel to a research center or do their work electronically. If our programs were to greatly expand, we should place advertisements and promote database training as a way of drawing attention to the resources that the Sawyer Library offers in support of these programs. For example, according to a recent survey (bizjournals.com 6/21/00), the fastest growth area in the East over the next 25 years is supposed to be Cape Cod, with an expected growth rate of 25.7% from

1999 to 2025. If our programs begin to reflect this growth rate, we might want to advertise our resources in the local paper and to redesign our web interface so that it draws students away from the web sites of other schools that offer courses on the Cape. As of Fall 2000, we have 78.6 FTE students enrolled in our programs on the Cape. This figure represents slightly under 2% of the total FTE enrollment. (see Enrollment)

- Dean College

    We should also continue to monitor the growth of the Dean College programs, to see at what point it would be advantageous to promote our resources more actively. As of Fall 2000, we have 33.2 FTE students enrolled on the Dean campus. (see Enrollment) Dean has just posted an advertisement for a new library director; this event may open avenues for promoting Sawyer Library resources on the Dean campus.

Program Expansion

The University may expand its degree offerings to include, for example, a Ph.D. program in Political Science or Sociology. These programs involve a number of research projects that will impact on the library's collections and document delivery services. We should increase visibility now, so that we will be better able to accommodate these new research requirements in the future. Specifically, this expansion will impact

- Serial subscriptions

- Licensing arrangements

- Monograph and other collections

- Document Delivery

- Interlibrary Loan

- Staff support for research consultations

- Technology

- Space

Appendix A - Timetable for Promotion

Event:	Activity	Timeframe: Fall	Spring	Summer
1	Place Ads in the **Suffolk Journal**	Sept - 3 weeks	Feb - 2 weeks	
2	Make available pens with URL and name			Reprint
3	Hold a No Fine Day		Last Day of Classes	
4	Conduct an Open House		During National Library Week	
5	Hang a TV that displays library ads		Install during Break	

Appendix B - Timetable for Positioning

Event:	Activity	Timeframe: Fall	Spring	Summer
1	Move the Library Sign		During Winter Break	
2	Set up a Suggestion Box Near the Windows		January	
3	Place a suggestion button on web page		When possible	
4	Design and Print a mouse pad with the library name on it.		Redesign	Reprint
5	Distribute a survey to each SSOM and CAS Dean on how well library meets needs of school			July
6	Revisit the library's mission on significance of phrase "informational resources"		Hold discussion	

Appendix C - Timetable for Learning

Event:	Activity	Timeframe: Fall	Spring	Summer
1	Conduct Formal Orientation Sessions	Around Labor Day		
2	Advertise Drop in library sessions	Sept	Feb	
3	Form a Student Library Committee	Sept/Oct		
4	Design and Print a mouse pad with the library name on it		Redesign	Reprint
5	Hold subject sessions on resources for specific disciplines Advertise through academic departments	3 times during semester	3 times during semester	
6	Distribute "Expectations" survey	Sept		

Appendix D - Timetable for Research

Event:	Activity	Timeframe: Fall	Spring	Summer
1	Send memos describing new databases	Ongoing	Ongoing	
2	Distribute and post faculty newsletters	Sept	Feb	
3	Conduct orientation sessions for faculty on specific databases	Nov	Mar	
4	Develop and post "New Book (and Video) Lists"	Oct	Feb	
5	Distribute to faculty a survey on their perceptions on student use of the library electronic resources			Aug/Sept

Appendix E - Cited References

(Catalog)   Suffolk University, College of Arts and Sciences, Sawyer School of
                Management, **Suffolk University Undergraduate and Graduate
                Academic Catalog 2000-2001**, "Mission Statement," 9.

(Enrollment)   Suffolk University, Enrollment Research and Planning, "Fall 2000 - Final
                Enrollments as of October 6, 2000," 1.

(Mission)   Suffolk University, Mildred F. Sawyer Library Strategic Plan July 1, 1999
                - June 30, 2002. "Mission Statement." Mildred F. Sawyer Library Web
                Page, November 13, 2000.
                < http://www.suffolk.edu/admin/sawlib/plandocs/stratplan.htm >

(FAQ)   Suffolk University, Office of Enrollment Research and Planning,
                "Frequently Asked Questions: Commonly Requested Data for the Fall
                1999 Semester." November 13, 2000.
                < http://www.suffolk.edu/admin/enrres/faq.html >

(bizjournals)   Thomas, G. Scott, "Cape Cod Will Set Population Pace in East:
                Projections Indicate Slow Growth Will Be Rule in Region,"
                bizjournals.com - demographics daily, June 21, 2000.
                < wysiwyg:// 56/http://www.bizjournals.com/journals/demographics/
                doc/2000/06/21/1.html >

MISSION STATEMENTS

BOWDOIN COLLEGE

Bowdoin College Library
Statement of Purpose and Goals
2002-2004

Purpose Statement

The Bowdoin College Library is an intellectual gathering place that fosters and enhances learning, education and research. The library's staff, services, resources, and collections advance the pursuit of knowledge and offer an information gateway to the world's ideas.

Core Values

1. We believe in the individual right to intellectual pursuit, free from censorship or violation of privacy.

2. We believe in nurturing the intellectual curiosity that leads to lifelong learning.

3. We believe in preserving connections to the past while embracing the challenges of the future.

4. We believe that in an ever-changing world, success depends upon flexibility, innovation and a constant reassessment of the needs of our community.

5. We believe that the strength of our library depends not only on its collections and services, but also on the quality of its staff.

6. We believe that the workplace should foster accomplishment, individual achievement and growth.

7. We believe in treating our colleagues and patrons with respect, honesty and good humor in recognition of a diverse community.

8. We believe that outstanding library service requires continuous collaboration, cooperation and clear communication.

Goals

Goal # 1:   Develop collections and provide optimal access to information resources to support the academic programs of the College.

Goal #2:   Offer library services and resources that enrich the curriculum and facilitate the research endeavors of faculty and students.

Goal #3:   Promote the use of information technologies and serve as a teaching laboratory where new resources and services are introduced, explored and developed.

Goal #4:   Enhance the educational experience of students at Bowdoin through teaching and promoting information literacy skills that are necessary to find, evaluate and use information effectively.

Goal #5:   Engage in a vital partnership with faculty members in the educational process.

Goal #6:   Promote the preservation and use of historical collections and archival records that serve the Bowdoin curriculum, College administrative programs and the scholarly community.

Goal #7:   Contribute to the intellectual, cultural, and recreational learning environment of the College beyond the classroom.

Goal #8   Build and continually develop a skilled staff equipped to meet the constantly changing needs of the Library and the campus community.

Goal # 9   Create a well-equipped and technologically up-to-date library facility providing all users and staff with an attractive, comfortable and safe environment conducive to work, study and learning.

Goal #10   Enhance access to information resources and services for faculty, students and staff through coordinated participation in regional, national and international resource sharing.

Goal #11   Promote the library profession and represent its ethics and standards through leadership on campus, in the profession and within the community at large.

Goal # 12   Serve as a resource for individuals outside the campus community, in coordination with the services of public and institutional libraries.

Goal # 1:   Develop collections and provide optimal access to information resources to support the academic programs of the College.

Supporting Statements:

A. The Library follows established collection evaluation, development and management policies when making acquisitions decisions in order to assure the formation of an appropriate and cohesive collection.

B. The Library's catalog services organize and describe scholarly resources based on national bibliographic standards.

C. The Library acquires, catalogs and processes materials in a timely and efficient manner, making the best use of staff, technology and financial resources.

D. The Library offers direct and mediated access to a wide array of print and electronic information resources and full-text databases.

E. Physical organization, management and maintenance of collections enhance access to and use of library materials.

F. The Library cooperates and collaborates with the Colby and Bates libraries to optimize collections, services and resources.

G. The Library uses conventional and innovative methods to preserve and protect its collections.

Goal #2:   Offer library services and resources that enrich the curriculum and facilitate the research endeavors of faculty and students.

Supporting Statements:

A. The Library assesses the structure and content of the curriculum, the research needs of faculty and students, and other campus educational activities to develop collections and instructional programs.

B. Interpretation of information resources and individual instruction in research methods support student and faculty research.

C. The Library develops portals, gateways and other interfaces that enhance access to information resources and library services.

D. Research guides in print and electronic format are available in a variety of subject areas.

E. Document delivery options reflect the most effective and broadest services available for providing timely and relevant support of research needs.

F. The Library delivers reserves in support of classroom assignments in a timely and efficient manner.

G. Library staff are committed to responding fully and respectfully to all inquiries and requests, either by providing relevant information or through appropriate referral.

<u>Goal #3:</u> **Promote the use of information technologies and serve as a teaching laboratory where new resources and services are introduced, explored and developed.**

The Library supports the "Bowdoin College Information Technology Plan," developed by the Information Technology (IT) Committee. The IT Committee serves as an executive committee for computing matters, advises the president and senior staff, and assists the CIS Director with planning and communications to the community. Members of the IT Committee include the Academic Dean and the Vice President for Finance and Administration who serve as co-chairs, the Director of CIS, the Librarian and the chairs of the Academic Computing, Administrative Computing and Student Computing committees and the Web Management Group. The plan emphasizes the collaborative responsibility and commitment among the Library, CIS, ETC, and other units to provide IT services for the Bowdoin community.

(See "Bowdoin College Information Technology Plan" at:
http://academic2.bowdoin.edu/it/html)

The Library endorses and actively participates in the efforts of the Educational Technology Center "to bring Bowdoin faculty together with staff trained in new educational and information technologies [ETC Charge: see http://academic.bowdoin.edu/etc/information/index.shtml] ."

The Library collaborates and cooperates with Computing and Information Services in its mission of "recognizing and satisfying present and future information technology needs of the Bowdoin Community in support of the College mission [CIS Mission Statement: see http://www.bowdoin.edu/cis/about/]."

Supporting Statements:

A. The Library develops and provides training programs that promote the effective use of information technology, in collaboration with ETC and CIS as appropriate.

B. The Library identifies, evaluates, selects and develops new technologies for teaching and research, in collaboration with CIS, ETC and faculty.

C. The Library provides state-of-the art facilities and equipment to access and present electronic information.

Goal #4:   **Enhance the educational experience of students at Bowdoin through teaching and promoting information literacy skills that are necessary to find, evaluate and use information effectively.**

Supporting Statements:

A. The Library's teaching and learning program builds progressively through a student's career beginning with basic skills taught in the first year and culminating with advanced skills for upper-level research projects.

B. The Library promotes, supports and integrates the teaching of information research skills into courses across the curriculum.

C. Course-related instruction introduces students to the information resources and research techniques of specific fields of study.

D. Each individual and group teaching experience in the library is an opportunity to build students' information gathering and assessment skills.

E. Students learn and develop computer literacy skills through their research activities in the library and their interaction with library staff.

Goal #5:   **Engage in a vital partnership with faculty members in the educational process.**

Supporting Statements:

A. Librarians participate in planning and develop services to support the academic programs of the College.

B. Librarian liaisons support faculty research, curriculum development and teaching, and alert faculty to library services and resources that are useful in their academic disciplines.

C. Librarians work with faculty to develop and assess library collections and services.

<u>Goal #6</u>: **Promote the preservation and use of historical collections and archival records that serve the Bowdoin curriculum, College administrative programs and the scholarly community.**

SUPPORTING STATEMENTS:

A. Library policies, procedures and facility design ensure the preservation and safety of irreplaceable and inherently unstable materials such as brittle books, photographs, and electronic data.

B. The Library promotes the integration of primary source material into the curriculum and informs the scholarly community of the unique intellectual and historical resources available at Bowdoin.

C. The Library helps the College community retrieve, interpret, and use historic College records through the Archives' management programs, library catalog, specialized services and finding aids.

D. The Library cooperates with other units of the College to preserve and promote the College's cultural heritage.

<u>Goal #7</u>: **Contribute to the intellectual, cultural, and recreational learning environment of the College beyond the classroom.**

SUPPORTING STATEMENTS

A. The Library sponsors and promotes cultural events, both independently and in coordination with other College programs and units.

B. The Library's circulating collections include materials intended for pleasure and recreation.

C. The Library provides materials for reading, viewing and listening to stimulate intellectual curiosity and promote self-education in areas of interest beyond the curriculum.

Goal #8   Build and continually develop a skilled staff equipped to meet the constantly changing needs of the Library and the campus community.

SUPPORTING STATEMENTS:

A. A staff well informed about the overall operations of the Library, working collaboratively and in coordination, facilitates the achievement of the Library's purpose and goals.

B. A staff well informed about the overall operations of the College and engaged in college-wide issues contributes to the effectiveness of both the College and the Library.

C. The Library recognizes that good staff morale contributes significantly in achieving the organization's goals and objectives.

D. A staff training and professional development program is a critical part of the library's operations; staff at all levels receive support in pursuit of such training and continuing education opportunities.

E. All staff receive adequate technical support and have access to state-of-the-art work stations appropriate to their responsibilities.

F. Staffing levels, assignments, and tools reflect the ongoing impact of changing workflow, technologies, and institutional priorities.

G. The Library recognizes the critical role of student employees in the provision of library services and acknowledges that students learn through their employment; consequently, the Library helps students develop their work skills through mentoring and job training.

Goal # 9   **Create a well-equipped and technologically up-to-date library facility providing all users and staff with an attractive, comfortable and safe environment conducive to work, study and learning.**

SUPPORTING STATEMENTS:

A. Appropriate and well maintained equipment and facilities ensure that faculty, staff, students, and visitors can access and use the library effectively.

B. Environmental controls in the library ensure safety and comfort and contribute to the preservation of library materials.

C. Ergonomically correct furnishings and lighting provide for the well-being of library users and staff.

D. Library facilities are designed to enhance instruction, individual study and collaborative learning, and to support cultural events.

E. Networked study and meeting spaces provide ubiquitous access to information technology.

F. Functional, flexible work space supports and reflects staff commitment to productivity, creativity and teamwork.

G. Safety and security measures are in place to protect library staff, users and collections.

Goal #10   **Enhance access to information resources and services for faculty, students and staff through coordinated participation in regional, national and international resource sharing.**

SUPPORTING STATEMENTS:

A. The Library participates in the ongoing development of the CBB Libraries Strategic Plan and supports its vision and goals.

B. Consortial agreements with other libraries, networks and cooperative programs ensure access to expanded reference, interlibrary loan and circulation services.

C. The Library joins with consortial partners to negotiate agreements with publishers, vendors and information providers that expand access to information and realize financial advantage.

Goal #11   **Promote the library profession and represent its ethics and standards through leadership on campus, in the profession and within the community at large.**

Supporting Statements:

A. The Library affirms and adheres to the Library Bill of Rights and its interpretations, the American Library Association Code of Ethics, the Society of American Archivists' Code of Ethics for Archivists, the ALA-SAA Joint Statement on Access, and the Association of College and Research Libraries (ACRL) Standard for Ethical Conduct for Rare Book, Manuscript and Special Collections Libraries and Librarians.

   See:
   "Library Bill of Rights" at http://www.ala.org/work/freedom/lbr.html#rights
   "American Library Association Code of Ethics" at
   http://www.ala.org/alaorg/oif/ethics.html
   "Society of American Archivists' Code of Ethics for Archivists" at
   http://www.archivists.org/governance/handbook/app_ethics.asp
   "ALA-SAA Joint Statement on Access to Original Research Materials" at
   http://www.ala.org/acrl/guides/ala-saa.html
   "Association of College and Research Libraries (ACRL) Standards for Ethical Conduct for Rare Book, Manuscript and Special Collections Libraries and Librarians" at http://www.ala.org/acrl/guides/rarethic.html

B. The Library encourages staff participation in professional organizations.

C. Library staff participate actively in campus committees and organizations.

D. The Library promotes librarianship as a career path.

Goal # 12   **Serve as a resource for individuals outside the campus community, in coordination with the services of public and institutional libraries.**

SUPPORTING STATEMENTS:

A. The Library supports the efforts of local, state and regional libraries to enhance their services to constituents.

B. The Library works with campus departments to develop library and technology use policies for visitors.

C. The Library offers selected services and resources for those outside the College community.

KRAEMER FAMILY LIBRARY
MISSION AND GOALS
2002/2003

8/12/02

The Kraemer Family Library's mission is to provide information services, sources, and instructional support services that are essential to the teaching, research, and service mission of the University of Colorado at Colorado Springs. To accomplish this mission, the library has the following goals and responsibilities:

Goal 1: Select, acquire, maintain, and preserve collections of print, non-print and electronic library resources with a diversity of perspectives suitable to teaching and learning programs, and to a more limited extent, the research programs of UCCS.

Core Strategies
1. Add guidelines for the selection of electronic resources to the library's collection development policy.

2. Review and update the collection development policy including the policies for the Kraemer Gift and expenditures of ICR funds.

3. Update and revise the allocation formula for the materials budget to address issues of allocations to new programs, changing programs, and concerns of faculty.

4. Strengthen the liaison program with academic departments.

5. Organize and process the backlog of archival material in the University Archives.

6. Continue to evaluate journals and electronic resources in terms of usage, cost, document delivery demand and value to the user, canceling and adding as needed and possible.

7. Identify and implement collection maintenance and preservation projects for print and non-print materials.

Performance Indicators

♦ By June 2003, the librarians will develop specific guidelines for the collection of various types of electronic resources and incorporate these guidelines into the collection development plan. (Librarians)

- By June 2003, the library will complete a review and update of the collection development plan. (Rita Hug and Librarians)

- By November 2002, the Library will review and revise the ICR expenditure policy. (Rita Hug and Librarians)

- By November 2002, the Library will conduct a survey of faculty to gain information to be used in provision of services and revision of the allocation process. (Mary Beth Chambers and Sue Byerley)

- By May 2003, implement the new allocation process, approved by the Library Advisory Committee that addresses issues of allocations to new programs and resolves issues with the existing formula. (Rita Hug)

- By December 2002 and June 2003, librarians will have contacted all faculty in their respective departments at least once a semester to discuss issues of collection development, making personal contact with all new faculty in those departments, and contacting all honorarium at least once. (Librarians)

- By June 2003, collect and evaluate cost data for existing electronic database and trial databases and evaluate possible additions or replacements including impact on print subscriptions. (Rita Hug)

- By December 2002, develop a specific collection development policy for the portion of the Kraemer Gift designated for materials. (Rita Hug and Librarians)

- By February 2003, shift microfilm and remaining map collections. (Teresa Strasner and Kathy Marshall)

- By February 2003, the backlog of archives materials will be reduced by at least 30% and all processed materials will be reflected appropriately in the archives primary finding aid, the alphabetical list of offices, schools, departments, publications, and names in record groups. (Mary Beth Chambers and Gudrun McCullum)

- By March 2003, install new version of Ariel software in Interlibrary Loan and investigate ways to implement the email function for delivery of articles. (Laurie Williams and Jennifer Quick)

- By March 2003, identify significant new uses of ILL's statistical programs to enhance the information available for acquisition purposes and investigate other ways to use ILL information in collection evaluation. (Laurie Williams and Jennifer Quick)

Goal 2: Process and organize print, non-print and electronic collections to ensure ease of access and encourage their use through quality reference service to on site and remote users.

Core Strategies

1. Develop procedures for cataloging and making accessible electronic resources.

2. Review and revise reference and use statistics to better report the use of services offered by the library both on site and at a distance.

3. Implement additional features of the III system to increase or improve access to materials through the library catalog.

4. Review use of OCLC services for cataloging and ILL to insure that we are using those services that maximize efficiency and access.

5. Evaluate customer service, hours of operations and reference hours with user input.

6. Provide automated access to uncataloged physical collections such as documents, microform sets and archives.

Performance Indicators

♦ By December 2002, establish access and cataloging links for electronic versions of journals received with print subscriptions. (Rita Hug, Mary Beth Chambers, Teresa Strasner, Sue Byerley)

♦ By September 2002, evaluate the use of "Serials Solutions" software to provide access to the titles purchased by the library. (Rita Hug and Sue Byerley)

♦ By December 2002, develop measurements to reflect the broader range of reference use and a means for collecting the data on these measurements. (Chris Martinez, Leslie Manning)

♦ By June 2003, explore OCLC's bibliographic notification services; and prepare for OCLC's CORC and web based products using CATME. (MaryBeth Chambers and Jackie Konselman)

♦ By December 2002, purchase and load cataloging records for netLibrary electronic books and catalog selected Colorado Documents. (MaryBeth Chambers, Jackie Konselman, Kathy Marshall)

♦ By March 2003, create a database of electronic database usage statistics, add counters to each page in the library's web site, and investigate statistics gathering procedures in III. (Sue Byerley & Christina Martinez)

- By June 2003, the library will have implemented the following III modules or features: Web Access Management; serials payment; millenium circulation; label printing; telnet software and full use of the 856 field for electronic resources. (Technical Services, Reference and Circulation Staff)

- By January 2003, create and distribute an electronic user survey on the Web and in print to evaluate user satisfaction with services, hours of operations, etc. (Judith Rice-Jones)

- By July 2003, integrate the use of the new campus ID card system into procedures at Circulation. (Circulation Staff)

Goal 3: **Provide bibliographical instruction programs, workshops and seminars that empower students, faculty and staff to obtain basic information literacy skills needed to become self-sufficient in finding, selecting, evaluating and using information that expands knowledge and understanding.**

Core Strategies
1. Develop web-based bibliographies and design electronic subject guides for disciplines/departments.

2. Increase the number of library instruction session and students reached by a minimum of 10% per year for each of the next two years through 2003.

3. Work with the Freshman Seminar to include library instruction in all sections.

4. Revise and update all library handouts adding them to the library web page.

5. Develop description of basic competency in information literacy.

6. Increase library staff knowledge and understanding of available electronic resources and promote and share that knowledge with faculty and students.

Performance Indicators
- By January 2003, electronic subject guides in at least one discipline for each subject librarian will be available on the library web site. (Librarians)

- By December 2002 and June 2003, the librarians will have contacted all faculty in their respective departments at least once a semester regarding the inclusion of library instruction/information literacy in their courses, making personal contact with all new faculty in those departments, and contacting all honorarium at least once. (Librarians)

- By November 2002, each section of the Freshman Seminar will have received a bibliographic instruction session. (Librarians)

♦ By January 2003, review and analyze information literacy programs at comparable campuses and draft a plan to enhance and update the library's information literacy (library instruction) program. (Judith Rice-Jones)

♦ By January 2003, all library handouts will be updated and on the library's web page including expanded information about library policy. To facilitate updating, librarians will learn Front Page software. (Cathy Mundy, Sue Byerley, Librarians)

♦ By September 2002, re-evaluate where we are in the "adopt" an electronic database program and determine the next steps. (Librarians)

♦ By January 2003, develop and implement a strategy for promoting the library's new electronic resources such as EBSCO, Wiley, SciDirect, etc. to faculty and students. (Chris Martinez, Librarians)

♦ By January 2003, study and evaluate GPO's web page, GPO Access, for use by the library and provide training to all staff. (Kathy Marshall)

Goal 4: **Foster cooperation and economies in the provision of information services through local, state and national partnerships with libraries, public institutions and private industry, in order to serve as UCCS' link to the global information network.**

Core Strategies
1. Participate in the evaluation of the use of Prospector, the Colorado global catalog.

2. Participate in the evaluation and further development of the CU Electronic Library.

3. Participate in the promotion, use and enhancement of the Colorado Virtual Library and statewide collection development.

4. Design and implement a public relations plan that informs the campus community of the library's role in community outreach as well as strengthen ties and cooperative programs with other libraries in Colorado Springs.

Performance Indicators
♦ By June 2003, the library will participate in the evaluation and enhancement of Prospector with the other Prospector partners. (Chris Martinez, Librarians)

♦ By June 2003, monitor the development of SWIFT, the new state ILL system, participating when feasible. (ILL)

♦ Beginning in September 2002, participate in campus activities and programming such as the Fall Fest and Club Fair to better inform the campus of our many services. (Judith Rice-Jones)

♦ By June 2003, in cooperation with the other CU campus libraries, investigate and recommend additional electronic resources for purchase and access at the four-campus level. (Rita Hug)

Goal 5: **Provide and maintain a library facility and infrastructure which is conducive to scholarship, research, and serious study; and which meets user, collection, and staff needs.**

Core Strategies

1. Participate in the resolution of remaining furniture, equipment and signage issues.

2. Provide timely displays according to established guidelines.

Performance Indicators

♦ By June 2003, develop and install a minimum of nine displays in the two cases. (Chris Martinez)

♦ By June 2003, resolve remaining furniture, equipment, signage and construction issues related to the new building. (Leslie Manning)

♦ During 2002-2003, report building maintenance issues on the designated form. (Library Staff)

♦ By January 2003, develop guidelines for donor recognition on the donor wall and implement those guidelines for current and past donors. (Leslie Manning)

♦ By September 2002, revise the library's signage policy to incorporate changes for the new building. (Sign Committee)

Goal 6: **Recruit and develop a diverse, self-reliant, self-directed library staff that is committed to achieving the mission of the library and the university.**

Core Strategies
1. Implement the Pay for Performance System for classified staff.

2. Encourage attendance at workshops or events that focus on diversity issues.

3. Follow the library faculty criteria for appointment, promotion and tenure.

4. Evaluate staffing patterns in light of changing services and operational demands.

5. Fill all vacant and new positions promptly with qualified, technologically experienced, diverse, self-directed and self-reliant individuals who are committed to service.

6. Ensure that each staff member accepts his/her responsibility for analyzing what skills they need to develop to better contribute to the mission of the library. Provide resources for staff and professional development.

Performance Indicators

♦ By March 2003, complete the annual evaluations and performance plans for classified staff under PPS will be complete. (Supervisors and classified staff)

♦ During 2002-2003, monitor and inform staff about changes to PPS. (Teresa Strasner, Jayne Lloyd)

♦ By June 2003, collect and analyze information on ongoing tenure issues. (Rita Hug, Suzanne Byerley)

♦ During 2002-2003, hire and train new staff for Circulation. (Chris Martinez and Judy Baranowski)

♦ By December 2002, establish an orientation program for new and existing student employees that addresses standardized expectations of training, a quality service attitude, how to deal with the public; employee etiquette, etc. (Judith Rice Jones, Lynn Holloway, Kathy Marshall)

♦ During 2002-2003, every library staff and faculty member will identify and attend at least one professional development activity (All Staff)

Goal 7: **Manage, administer, and expand the library's resources effectively and efficiently.**

Core Strategies

1. Seek outside sources of funding for the campus Capital Campaign.

2. Seek non-gift sources of new funding for the library.

3. Implement new contract for library microform reader-printer machines.

4. Document policies and procedures to ensure continuity following staff departures and retirements.

5. Continue to explore the potential of PeopleSoft and implement enhancements and features appropriately.

6. Participate in the campus IRMS budgeting process.

7. Complete the annual and three year planning documents for the library and participate in the campus planning process.

Performance Indicators

♦ By June 2003, the library will establish a development committee and with the CU Foundation, assist in raising dollars for the campus' Capital Campaign. (Leslie Manning)

♦ By September 2002, complete the three year contract for the library's microform reader-printer machines. (Jayne Lloyd)

♦ In 2002-2003, continue to participate in training and planning for IRMS, the multiyear budgeting process. (Jayne Lloyd, Rita Hug, Leslie Manning)

♦ By December 2002, establish the guidelines for Kraemer gift expenditures. (Rita Hug and Leslie Manning)

♦ By June 2003, identify a grant source and apply for funding for library collections. (Librarians)

♦ By June 2003, apply for state grant dollars, technology fee dollars and other similar funding opportunities. (Rita Hug, Chris Martinez, Leslie Manning)

♦ During 2002-2003, continue the documentation of policies and procedures for the Technical Services Units. (Technical Services Staff)

♦ By February 2003, integrate more fully the use of A-Card in acquisitions processes. (Cindy Allen)

♦ By February 2003, collect input from library staff and develop the first draft of the three year library plan. By March 2003, the final three year plan will be available. (Planning Committee)

♦ By August 2002, finalize the vision, mission and values statement of the Kraemer Family Library. (Planning Committee)

- By June 2003, the library will complete a review and update of the collection development plan. (Rita Hug and Librarians)

- By November 2002, the Library will review and revise the ICR expenditure policy. (Rita Hug and Librarians)

- By November 2002, the Library will conduct a survey of faculty to gain information to be used in provision of services and revision of the allocation process. (Mary Beth Chambers and Sue Byerley)

- By May 2003, implement the new allocation process, approved by the Library Advisory Committee that addresses issues of allocations to new programs and resolves issues with the existing formula. (Rita Hug)

- By December 2002 and June 2003, librarians will have contacted all faculty in their respective departments at least once a semester to discuss issues of collection development, making personal contact with all new faculty in those departments, and contacting all honorarium at least once. (Librarians)

- By June 2003, collect and evaluate cost data for existing electronic database and trial databases and evaluate possible additions or replacements including impact on print subscriptions. (Rita Hug)

- By December 2002, develop a specific collection development policy for the portion of the Kraemer Gift designated for materials. (Rita Hug and Librarians)

- By February 2003, shift microfilm and remaining map collections. (Teresa Strasner and Kathy Marshall)

- By February 2003, the backlog of archives materials will be reduced by at least 30% and all processed materials will be reflected appropriately in the archives primary finding aid, the alphabetical list of offices, schools, departments, publications, and names in record groups. (Mary Beth Chambers and Gudrun McCullum)

- By March 2003, install new version of Ariel software in Interlibrary Loan and investigate ways to implement the email function for delivery of articles. (Laurie Williams and Jennifer Quick)

- By March 2003, identify significant new uses of ILL's statistical programs to enhance the information available for acquisition purposes and investigate other ways to use ILL information in collection evaluation. (Laurie Williams and Jennifer Quick)

Goal 8: Collaborate with other campus units in the development of a coordinated strategy for information management, information services, information literacy, and general education.

Core Strategies

1. Work collaboratively with other residents of the "Information Commons" to insure that users are informed of, trained for, and receive effective information services from Reference, Computer labs and Multimedia development in the new facility.

2. Participate in the campus' general education requirements planning process and determine the library's role in any new general education requirement plan.

Performance Indicators

♦ By June 2003, the library will complete campus planning requirements as requested by the Campus Planning Committee. (Planning Committee)

♦ By June 2003, develop specific assessment measures for information literacy that can be used with the general education requirements. (Judith Rice-Jones)

♦ During 2002-2003, refine the operations of the Information Commons and address any issues that arise. (User Services)

♦ By January 2003, work with Information Technology and Disability Services to fully implement the assistive technology lab. (Sue Byerley, Cathy Mundy)

♦ By June 2003, develop policies, services, and instructional materials to address the needs of extended studies and on-line students. (Chris Martinez)

POSITION DESCRIPTIONS

Public Services Librarian Responsibilities

Supervisor:
Library Director; annual review August/September; monthly & annual statistical reports; annual leave is approved as far in advance as possible; sick leave should be called in to both public services staff and library administrative staff.

Hours:
Approximately 40 hours per week; schedule is flexible & negotiable, but building opening and closing is usually the responsibility of public services personnel.

Management of Public Services Division:
Includes circulation, reference, interlibrary loans, and user instruction; circulation & ILL should not occupy too much time as long as experienced personnel remain; a part-time personnel budget is established each fiscal year by the library director and is used to produce a work schedule; reference desk is staffed with professional librarians, a few experienced classified staff, and a couple of capable part-time employees; user instruction is usually by appointment; faculty should be expected to provide advanced notice and expectations; LBMD2001 is offered in two sections, one hour per week each, currently scheduled for 8am Wednesday and 11am Thursday; an LBMD2001 syllabus is available and other library staff can be brought in to cover special subject matter.

Reference Collection Management:
The reference collection is kept current mostly by standing orders; shelf management for all print materials except periodicals and government documents is handled by circulation staff; reference materials selection is usually done in collaboration with professional staff subject liaisons.

Electronic Database Selection:
Electronic databases are mostly subscriptions; selection, continuation, and deselection should be done in collaboration with professional staff subject liaisons; license agreements and specifications are monitored by the PSL.

Departmental Liaison:
Each professional librarian works with faculty in designated disciplines (usually three) to develop collections and services; to the extent possible, these disciplines are assigned based on subject expertise.

Personnel Supervision:
The PSL supervises a staff of two full-time classified staff as well as numerous student and part-time workers; annual performance reviews are required for all classified staff; all classified staff and part-time workers must complete monthly (semi-monthly for extra labor) timesheets.

Library Communications / Public Relations:
All informational materials relating to library services, whether in print, electronic, or other formats, are produced by public services staff in collaboration with the director and/or other appropriate library personnel.

Other:
Because of our small staff, we are all called on occasionally to do things outside of and in addition to the above list of duties and responsibilities. Often, these will be voluntary, but sometimes not. Due consideration should always be given to these requests or assignments, and they should be undertaken with the same attitude of professionalism applied to other tasks.

Displays & Events Coordinator, 2001-02

Responsibilities

1. **Plan and arrange library displays which highlight or complement events, themes and issues at Goshen College.**

   Opportunities for coordination of library displays include (but are not limited to) the following:

   - Upcoming campus events – speakers, programs, etc.
   - Commemorative dates of particular interest to the college community and/or the library's services, e.g. Black History Month, National Poetry Month, National Library Week, significant dates related to Christian and/or Anabaptist history, etc.
   - Thematic programs associated with various departments and offices, e.g. year-long General Education focus
   - Issues, topics and trends of importance to the student body and faculty – as addressed in campus publications, convocations, chapels, and various informal gatherings and venues

2. **Solicit and develop ideas for library-sponsored events.**

   Specific proposals should be presented to the Library Director, librarians and/or representatives from other departments who would be involved in planning or underwriting these events.

3. **Coordinate and oversee signage and ad hoc informational displays in the library.**

   This would ensure that at least one person as an overall sense of what is posted where in the library and can work towards more consistency in the placement and design of library signage.

Resources

1. **Funding**

   A specific budget has not (yet) been set for these activities. However, the Displays and Events Coordinator will have access to some funding for materials and supplies through the library's general budget. Additionally, the Coordinator should seek out opportunities to share costs with other interested departments and institutions. For instance, if a display corresponds to an author visit, the Coordinator should contact the department who is sponsoring the visit to discuss and negotiate support for the library to purchase the author's works. The Coordinator should also cultivate contacts and relationships with outside institutions – educational, cultural, social and corporate – which might be interested in partnering with the library on programs and events.

2. **Staff**

   The Displays and Events Coordinator may request assistance from the other librarians, library staff members and student workers in designing, setting up and tearing down displays. (Direct supervisors should be consulted first to coordinate the request with preexisting priorities and workload.)

Swarthmore College Position Description
OUTREACH, INSTRUCTIONS COORDINATOR, AND REFERENCE SERVICES LIBRARIAN

Dept.: Swarthmore College Libraries
Reports to: Head of Reference
Date: March 2000
FTE: .8

BASIC FUNCTION AND RESPONSIBILITY

The Outreach, Instructions Coordinator and Reference Services Librarian is responsible for developing services and instructional programming for the immediate Swarthmore College community and beyond. The librarian will work specifically with the Dean's Office, particularly those people in academic advising, with Human Relations and with other appropriate offices to develop programming which enhances life skills in the areas of information literacy and with various non-campus constituencies such as local schools and community based programs. This Librarian also serves as the subject specialist for Education, Modern Languages and African Studies and is responsible for services to the BCC and other cultural centers on campus. As a member of the public services team the Outreach, Instructions Coordinator and Reference Services Librarian works scheduled times at the reference desk, participates in shared management of the public services department and shared responsibility for selection of reference sources including digital sources.

ESSENTIAL DUTIES

Instructional Program Development

• Responsible for leadership for and coordination of the library's instruction program. Specifically, assesses the needs for various types of instructional programming including workshops, course integrated instruction and documentation for all the library's constituencies and works with faculty, administration and colleagues to deliver that programming. Serve as a resource for library colleagues participating in library instruction and help design and implement instruction activities. Serves as spokesperson for advocating for library's instructional mission and works towards integrating information literacy skills as an essential piece of the undergraduate curriculum. Devise strategies for promoting and marketing instruction to faculty and students on campus.

• Responsible for developing and coordinating the implementation of first year orientation program for library and coordinating with Dean's office. Conducts assessment of library orientation program. Facilitates the January Academic Skills Workshop. Conducts assessment of first year library orientation programs. Promotes library instruction for all primary distribution courses.

• Provide leadership in developing workshop series on use of the on-line catalog and database services through the library's Innopac system, Internet and other electronic resources. Serve as a resource for library colleagues participating in library instruction

Outreach and Instructions Librarian

and help design and implement instruction activities. Develop and present workshops for all library users, students, staff, and faculty that respond to a diversity of cultural needs, learning styles and subject areas represented by the campus community.

• Identifies needs and sets priorities for the library's print/Web documentation. Included in documentation are general instructional guides, research guides, course guides and database guides. Coordinates the creation of content for these guides – working closely with the Digital Services Librarian and subject specialists – and insures the adequate maintenance of the guides.

• Keeps abreast of current scholarship in educational theory, undergraduate teaching and library instruction in order to inform program development. Responsible for the continuing introduction of emerging technologies & sound instructional resources to the College community.

Outreach Services

• Assesses the information needs of potential library user community and develops programming which will address those needs.

• Develops and seeks funding for outreach initiatives which enable members of local communities to more effectively acquire and use information resources. Examples include, but are not limited to projects with K-12, disadvantaged youths or Swarthmore's ABC program.

• Works with existing programs such as Learning for Life, Upward Bound, Community Service Learning Office to evaluate specific needs of Swarthmore staff and create and deliver programming to meet those needs.

• Serve as an interface to the Dean's office and students with disabilities and recommend to the library administration means of addressing those students' needs. Stays abreast of technological developments which provide effective means for students with disabilities to engage in library research.

• Strengthen library presence with different social centers on campus, the *Women's Resource Center, Black Cultural Center, Intercultural Center and Academic Support* and other campus supportive services including the *Writing Center.*

Library Subject Specialist

• Provides in-depth support to Modern Language and Education departments and the African Studies program. Works closely with faculty to understand the department's curriculum, major requirements, and areas of research in order to anticipate and meet service and collection needs.

• Provides in-depth consultation and research assistance as needed to faculty and students in the disciplines. May do significant literature searches for faculty to provide them with overviews of literature in particular areas. Works with students to help them develop researchable theses or "term paper" topics - requires a thorough understanding of the library's holdings (as well as those in Bryn Mawr and Haverford).

• Provides instruction in research methods and resources in the Modern Languages and Literature and Education in collaboration with teaching faculty or through independent workshops in order to provide students with knowledge to be independent and skilled researchers. Designs, assesses and implements instructional series from basic to advanced, appropriate to the level of the students and the course. This may include, but is not limited to, course integrated instruction, workshops, online tutorials and documentation, library orientations and individual student consultations.

• Works closely with Language Lab staff to assist faculty with the integration of information technology into the curriculum and research. For example, may be asked to help design Web pages of resources; develop online guides to the research in particular areas; locate primary source materials available in digital format; or assist with the creation of databases of primary source material. Participates in professional development activities in order to stay abreast of new developments in Modern Languages computing.

• Works with Education faculty to coordinate the collections of the library with those of the Educational Materials Laboratory.

Coordinates Services to the BCC and ICC

• Works with Black Studies Committee and staff of the BCC to plan collections and services of the BCC. Develops bridging program to ensure that students who use the BCC can effectively use the other Swarthmore libraries.

• Selects materials for the Black Cultural Center to maintain it as a vibrant and effective collection.

Serves as a Member of the Library's Public Services Team

• Provides primary reference support at McCabe Library. Shifts may include weekend or evening hours. Provides assistance to faculty, students, staff, as well as non-Swarthmore library patrons, in formulating research strategies and identifying appropriate information resources in print, digital and other media.

• Analyzes patron needs, works with patrons to understand their actual (rather than stated) information need, and helps the patron translate that need into research strategies which take best advantage of the resources at hand.

• Interprets the Swarthmore libraries for the library patron; assists them in navigating both real (physical) and digital space in order to locate appropriate materials.

• Participates in public services meetings and shared management of the department which includes strategic and operational planning for public services.

• Participates in shared collection development decisions for general reference sources in all formats. Evaluates publications and products for their quality, potential use, scholarly content and usability. Requires an understanding of existing collections, knowledge of competing products, and understanding of potential user needs.

• Proposes innovative references services which will enhance and expand departmental programs and goals. Expands and improves existing reference services and reference-area projects.

Outreach and Instructions Librarian

Selects Materials for McCabe Library's Modern Languages, African Studies Collections and Education Department

• Develops the Modern Languages, African Studies, and Education collection to ensure its pertinence and availability to all students and faculty in the Modern Languages and Education departments and African Studies program for their educational and research needs. Knows and uses professionally accepted criteria and resources to select materials in support of the collection development mission and to evaluate the collection in connection with related units of the College. This requires an in-depth understanding of evolving structure and scholarship in the disciplines (for example, growth in interdisciplinarity), a knowledge of at least two modern languages, as well as maintaining an awareness of new publications in the field. Selects materials from a number of sources including the approval program, publishers' catalogs, pre-publication alerts, journal book reviews, and Choice cards. Selection depends upon a complex evaluation that weighs various factors including relevancy to curriculum or faculty research, scope of library holdings in the same subject, presence of material under consideration in another Tri-College collection, reputation of the author in the discipline and reputation of the publisher in the discipline.

• Anticipates and identifies developments in the field of print and electronic resources and collection management as related to the Modern Languages and Literature, African Studies, and Education in order to support continuous improvement. Using various reviewing media and other bibliographic tools and apparatus, identifies and acquires materials to support curricular and research needs. Notifies faculty of materials of interest to them and/or their students. Keeps abreast of disciplinary trends as well as the changing scholarly communication patterns within Modern Languages and Literature, African Studies, and Education to ensure that the library collection is responsive to the interests of faculty and students. Develops a thorough understanding of the Modern Languages and Literature, African Studies, and Education key monographs publishers and major journals and monitors these publishers in order to acquire materials in a timely manner and make faculty aware of new resources in their discipline.

• Continually studies the demographics and needs of the population served by the McCabe Library, and considers those factors when making materials selections. Regularly evaluates and assesses the collection to identify areas in which more materials are needed. Researches circulation patterns of the materials in relation to the population served in order to assess the value of the collection and the needs of its users. Reviews interlibrary lending transactions to identify further materials for acquisition or areas for collection development.

• Selects, using professionally accepted criteria, appropriate Web sites for inclusion on Modern Languages, African Studies, and Education-related Web pages. Coordinates with tri-college (Bryn Mawr and Haverford) colleagues in development of these pages.

• Working with faculty, makes decisions regarding the de-acquisition (total removal) or re-disposition of Modern Language and Literature, African Studies, and Education materials into remote storage. Plans for and selects less-essential collection pieces for transfer into remote storage facility. Develops policy and makes decisions as to replacement or removal from collection based on content, historical value and other variable factors.

Outreach and Instructions Librarian

• Demonstrates initiative in developing projects outside the immediate day-to-day responsibilities and operations of the library. Such projects may involve seeking external grant funding. Some examples might include working with students in the Chester community to introduce them to computer based research; developing digital collections of unique materials in the Swarthmore libraries; developing new programmatic directions for the College's libraries.

INTERNAL / EXTERNAL RELATIONSHIPS:

• Works with Dean's Office to ensure library is meeting needs of disabled students.

• Works with faculty, community and social action leaders to develop and implement outreach programs. Communicates frequently with faculty regarding policies, services, collections (purchases and removals), databases, etc. Meets at least once per semester with each department and proactively engages faculty in the development of services. As subject specialist, works with faculty and students to develop collections and assist in research projects.

• Assists students, faculty, staff, and non-Swarthmore library patrons in the use of all aspects of the library as part of the public services/reference group both at the reference desk and in individual consultations or in instructional settings.

• Works with Associate College Librarian to determine how users' needs would be best served by either withdrawing materials from the collection or transferring materials to a remote storage site.

• Works with Digital Services Librarian, academic computing coordinators, language lab staff, (Tri-Co Mellon 2 staff) and other subject specialists to identify curricular support projects which might benefit from library professionals' expertise. Works with faculty to support implementation of these projects.

• Develops and maintains effective liaisons and plans cooperative projects with relevant professionals in other organizations in order to promote cooperative opportunities. Collaborates with public service library staffs at Bryn Mawr and Haverford libraries to coordinate shared collection development and remote storage projects as well as other management projects.

• Supervised by the Head of Reference. Acts independently with little supervision. Has wide choice in selection, development and coordination of methods within a broad framework of general policies. Consults with supervisor on unusual problems and policy setting. Actions, recommendations and decisions are subject to general review.

TECHNICAL SKILLS:

• Demonstrates an understanding of educational theory and its applicability to library instruction.

• Demonstrates an understanding of Modern Languages and Education literature, how research in the different disciplines supported at Swarthmore is communicated and disseminated

• Demonstrates knowledge of key issues related to information access and management.

• Demonstrates an understanding of library materials organization and classification.

Outreach and Instructions Librarian

- Maintains proficiency with general computing applications including: MS Word, Eudora, Netscape, file translation software and basic system software.

- Maintains proficiency with operations of Macintosh and Dell hardware in order to support both public use of computers as well as lending and access services hardware.

INTERACTIVE SKILLS:

- Demonstrates a strong service orientation; willing to go to great lengths to ensure that patrons and colleagues are able to access and use the library's resources, both traditional and digital in an effective manner. Demonstrates a commitment to promoting library services to the academic community. Helps users articulate their needs, so that the problem solving process can begin. Assists users in learning how to find the information or resolve the problems in an effort to enable them to solve their own problems.

- Thinks creatively and critically about programs, services, and resources in order to provide the best possible environment to support student and faculty library use. Works with other staff members to facilitate broader input on the above.

- Deals effectively with institution's cultural environment and various levels of expectations of both patrons and college administration in order to provide relative equity of resources in support of the assigned subject disciplines and programs.

- Exhibits an approachable and open style in personal interactions with patrons and colleagues and able to communicate with a wide range of patrons and colleagues; is collaborative in decision making; and cooperative in responding to requests from colleagues and supervisors. Possess strong verbal communication skills and maintain composure and ease in speaking in both group and individual settings, even under high levels of stress.

- Accomplishes tasks with a high level of professionalism, maintaining composure, even under high levels of stress; working effectively with other members of the Library staff.

- Able to stay focused and manage time effectively to accomplish goals and objectives. Works independently with little or no supervision. Must also juggle competing priorities well, and exhibit good judgment in setting those priorities. Position is engaged in problem solving, project work and daily functions at the same time. Must know one's limits and be able to distinguish when to handle an issue and when to escalate a problem to, the computing center, or others. Ability to organize work, keep track of ongoing and one-time tasks, and involve others is critical.

- Understands and abides by high standard of professional ethics, in order to ensure the integrity of the organization. For example, has access to individual borrowing records and other confidential and private information.

- Must preserve patrons' freedom of inquiry without personal judgment. Attempt to provide access to balanced viewpoints, and not to explicitly censor viewpoints or materials in building collections or directing patrons to information.

- Continuously seeks to enhance technical skills through formal (workshops, conferences, etc.) and informal (peer consulting, research, etc.) mechanisms. Displays great initiative in continually teaching oneself through exploration of systems, research or documentation.

Outreach and Instructions Librarian

- Engages in a routine review of periodicals and other subscriptions in order to free up funds for new purchases, either digital or traditional. Must balance role as advocate for departmental needs with mission and budget of the library.

- Coordinates with counterparts at Bryn Mawr and Haverford Colleges in order to develop joint collection development, collection retention and storage policies.

- Formulates goals and priorities for the development of new digital collections in the Modern Languages and Literature, African Studies and Education (including online databases and full-text electronic journals) in order to strengthen and broaden collections.

- Works with colleagues at the University of Pennsylvania and with African Studies Program Coordinator to determine priorities for expenditures utilizing African Studies Grant from U.S. DOE. Maintains records of expenditures and writes annual report for grant.

Tri-College Cooperation

- Collaborates with Tri-College librarians in order to exchange information, coordinate activities, and negotiate policies with regard to instruction, collection development, or other areas of common interests, while ensuring proposed projects and initiatives are feasible within the tri-college infrastructure. For example, negotiates which institution will be responsible for a new edition of an author's collected works.

- Coordinates tri-college Modern Languages and Literature, African Studies and Education collection development with librarians at Bryn Mawr and Haverford. Researches and determines, with the librarians, which electronic resources would best serve tri-college patrons in terms of support for faculty instruction and research as well as for educational and research support for students.

PROFESSIONAL ACCOMPLISHMENT AND DEVELOPMENT

- Contributes actively to the profession in a variety of ways. These should include demonstrable accomplishment in at least one of several areas detailed below. Over time the incumbent should demonstrate an increasing level of professional accomplishment.

  - Engages in research in the field and publication of the results and/or disseminating results through other means such as conference presentations. Research can take many forms but should ideally be on topics that would enhance the library's service.

  - Participates in local, state, or national organizations through committee work or by serving in a leadership position in those organizations.

  - Participates in conferences as speaker and/or assisting with program development.

- Actively seeks out opportunities for professional growth including the following:

  - Attends national or regional conferences and workshops on topics related to one's immediate responsibilities; reports back to the libraries about conference content.

  - Attends national or regional conferences and workshops on which allow one to assume new responsibilities.

Outreach and Instructions Librarian

• Continuously seeks to enhance understanding of evolving scholarly communication processes and librarianship and allied fields. Displays initiative seeking opportunities for professional growth and venues for contributing to the growth of the profession.

• As member of the Library Department, anticipates and recognizes tasks which need to be done and willingly undertake such tasks in order to ensure a library which most effectively serves its patrons' needs. (Ex. shelving books at the semester's end). Takes positive action when one identifies a problem by contributing to its solution.

• Possesses a sense of humor and recognizes that we are all in the same "boat."

EDUCATION AND TRAINING:

• MLS in library and/or information science from an ALA accredited library school with a concentration in reference services.

• Advanced or undergraduate degree in Education or social services highly preferable.

• Two or more years experience providing both group and individual instruction. Versed in educational theory including methodologies, learning styles. Well developed teaching skills and passion for teaching.

• Evidence of ability work effectively with initiative and creativity within a collegial framework. Evidence of project development experience is highly desirable.

• Demonstrated in-depth understanding of scholarly communication in the liberal arts and familiarity with collection development tools and strategies.

• Ability to work effectively with colleagues, students, faculty and staff in a rapidly changing, complex, and diverse environment, where there is considerable scope for planning and implementing new program initiatives.

• Excellent oral and written communication skills, analytical and problem solving skills, and interpersonal skills.

• Evidence of strong service orientation.

PROMOTION PLANS

How to promote

Current ways:
- Newsletter (paper & electronic)
- Posters and Bookmarks - Slogan
- Handouts/Services guides
- Display cases
- TD articles
- TD ads
- Table tents (Library, Olmsted, Hubbell)
- Campus Activities calendar (weekly email)
- On Campus articles
- Library Web Page

Suggestions:
- Orientation/activity fair/health fair tables (any time campus groups have representatives)
- Work with Wanda Everage about student connection opportunities
- Promotional items: computer key board card, pens, t-shirts,
- Wall Calendar
- Request Library contact information be added to syllabus
- FYS – Librarian contact letters
- Kiosks – lobby for academic and/or DRINK
- List serv for library announcements only
- Page about the library services in the D-Book
- K-12 Outreach/promotion (1) go to them to discuss information literacy (2) promote librarianship
- Alumni Update publication
- Community (guest services) meeting night
- Promote facility space to students through SAB

Priority

1. Work on Service Guides to send out in the form of a personal letter to all FT faculty
   - Kathy W & Kathy L will work on layout and database
   - Marcia & Liga will work on content
2. Poster and bookmarks
   - Kathy L is working on a new look/slogan

** The remaining priorities/timetable/assignments will be assigned later after Rod can review the list.**

Events or potential events for 2003-2004

- Banned Book Week – Sept 20-27
- International Writing Program Discussion – Sept 11
- Coleman Book Discussion/signing – October
- School of Ed. – Book Week - November
- National Library Week – April 18-24
- Bucksbaum related events - ?

- Black History Month – February
- Women's History Month – March
- Lobby Artwork (with veto power)(collaboration)
- Music Group in to perform
- Poetry Readings
- Open Mic Night

Services to Promote

General Services at the start of school for (1) faculty and (2) students

New Services for potential promotion
- Guest services: public, alumni, local schools, local colleges
- Rooms Pilot Project
- Drake Digital Repository

Internal Promotion to work on a friendly and helpful atmosphere for student employees
(potential Student acknowledgement like Student of the Semester Honor)

How do we (the library) want to be perceived?

- User-friendly, warm & welcoming

- Providing services, information (electronic, book, journal, web-based), and technology to on campus and off campus (including distance education)

- Research services

- Space for study, classes, and conference/meetings

Goals (big picture outcomes) / Objects (specific & quantifiable)

Goals (big picture outcomes)	Objects (specific & quantifiable)
Facility availability	# of classes, meetings # of building entrances
Provide quality service	# of people that access books, jn, dbase, web # of ILL/DD # of reserves, e-reserves, e-books, etc
User-friendly	LIBQUAL results Internal administered user surveys "mystery" user
Research Oriented	# of reference staff/hours # of one-on-one appointments liaisons # of ILL/DD # of faculty scholarly publications # of gov't doc

Current Activities:

- Work with Wanda Everage about student connection opportunities
    - Marcia & group to meet with Wanda on July 22

- Orientation/activity fair/health fair tables (any time campus groups have representatives)
    - Claudia and Kathy L. to contact groups

- Request Library contact information be added to syllabus
    - Put a note on the service guide/perspectus about adding library link & #s

- Kiosks – lobby for academic and/or DRINK
    - Susan to work on who to approach about the Starbucks in the lobby.
    - Maybe start on special occasions – beginning of term, finals, Sunday evenings

- Page about the library services in the D-Book
    - Kathy W to check on possibility and price

- Displays/Artwork and music/poetry presentations – policy and contacts
    - Kathy W. & Kathy L

Fall activities:

- Promotional items: computer key board card, pens, t-shirts,
    - Marcia to check with supplier about pricing
    - Kathy W. also has knows of a contact person for shirts
    - Perhaps look to 2nd sponsor to help cover costs.

- Wall Calendar – goes along with promotional item but yet will take more work – work on during the fall for possibly a calendar year or 18+ month calendar
    - Kathy to work on photos as part of poster/bookmarks
    - Marcia to check with supplier about pricing

- First Year Students – Librarian contact letters – work on in the Fall
    - Follow up at the 2nd semester with all Freshman – approx 800

- List serv for library announcements only
    - Need to continue to check into this for a late Fall start date.

- Alumni Update publication (twice a year ?)
    - Susan to submit items to Marketing Dept.

- Community (guest services) meeting night
    - Kris

- Promote facility space to students through SAB
    - Wait until after meeting with Wanda to see if there are some new ideas.

- Student Acknowledgement Award – Start working on details for a semester award
    - Kathy L & Kris

Spring/Summer 2004 activities:

- K-12 Outreach/promotion (1) go to them to discuss information literacy (2) promote librarianship

MEDIA RELATIONS MANUAL

media guide
simple steps to media shorts

Contents

**Who to Contact if You
Have News** 2

**Some Advice to Ensure a
Successful Process** 2

**Ten Easy Steps to Promoting
Your Event** 3

**Should the Media
Come a Calling** 3

**When You Are Talking to a
Reporter** 4

Tools of the Trade 4

Examples 5

Frequently Asked Questions 6

**Appendix A:
Ad Rates and Sizes** 7

**Appendix B:
Superstar Stories** 8

**Appendix C:
Templates for Fliers and
Brochures** 9

November 1, 2000

Hello Southern Oregon University...

The Office of Marketing and Public Relations consists of the Director of Marketing, the Public Relations Coordinator, and the Student Assistant. In the serious business of marketing, representing, and promoting the University, our office believes that a sense of style is optimal, a sense of humor, necessary. We are attempting to carry over that simple philosophy into this guide, the purpose of which is to serve as a reference tool. It is written based on our personal experiences integrated with the wise contributions from colleagues in the field. We hope that you will find the organization accessible and the information useful.

Our office is available for consultation at any time, so don't hesitate to call us at 552-6421 or check our web site at www.sou.edu/marketing.

SOUTHERN
OREGON
UNIVERSITY

Just leave the driving to us
Who to Contact if You Have News

If you have an item that you think would be interesting to the general public, or an event you need to promote, don't hesitate to call our office (552-6421). The public relations coordinator will first meet with you to get all of the pertinent information, consider the best way to disseminate your information to the media, and brainstorm promotion ideas. If you are short on time, you may also email the "what, when, where, who, and how" to us at news_stu@sou.edu, or fax the info to 552-6280. We will get in touch with you and work to get the news out as soon as possible.

We are also collecting information on a regular basis for our "Media Big Fish File," a comprehensive collection of campus story possibilities for use upon media request and for on-campus publications like the faculty and staff newsletter, the legislative newsletter, and the *Southern Oregonian*. If you have activities, submissions, research projects, publications, awards, or a bizarre hobby, contact us immediately. Together we can discuss the best way to make the most of your story.

Some Advice to Ensure a Successful Process

Before coming to visit our office, we recommend that you read the following points and, if you are organizing event publicity, the "Ten Easy Steps to Promoting Your Event" guide that follows. It will make our interaction and discussion time shorter and more productive.

- Please give us as much advance notice as possible. If you are helping to plan an event on campus, we ask that you notify us at least ten weeks before the event, if possible. If you have received an honor or award, notify us as soon as the award is announced.

- You can never provide too much information. Background details and facts are essential to the production of a good news release, and the more you give us, the better informed the media will be.

- Please make sure that the information you supply is completely accurate. It is crucial to the University's reputation that our office is regarded as a source of 100 percent reliable news. Sometimes the release of inaccurate information is unavoidable, in which case a correction must be sent without delay.

- If you are unsure your news or accomplishment merits media attention, please call Marketing and Public Relations. Here are a few questions to ask yourself:

  Is the item current?

  Does the item play into any recent trends in the media?

  Does it appeal to a wide audience?

  Would you want to read about it in the news?

We cannot ensure that your news will be covered. Despite our best efforts, you may not see any mention of your news or event in the media. Journalists do not, unfortunately, cover all news items they receive. There is simply not enough time or space to do so. To show our respect to the journalists we work with, we send only newsworthy items and the releases appropriate to their beats. We issue one follow-up call to the journalists to make certain they have received our release information. If they do not respond, we respect their decision not to cover that particular piece of news.

2

TEN Easy Steps to Promoting Your Event

Consider your audience.
What is the primary goal of your promotional campaign? Do you want to increase attendance at the event, or do you simply want coverage? Who would be your ideal audience and how can you reach them? These questions will assist you greatly in promoting your event.

Direct mail.
Direct mail is one of the fastest and most efficient ways to contact a large population in a small amount of time. Databases of addresses for SOU alumni, friends, and affiliates may be available for direct mailing through the SOU Foundation. You may send information to faculty and staff on campus by filling out a Mail Services work order.

Fliers.
Fliers are an inexpensive and effective means of creating a visible identity for your event. Because of this, fliers should be of high quality and contain all of the relevant information about your event. The Office of Marketing and Public Relations has templates available for the creation of fliers. Just as important as the creation is the distribution. Fliers should be numerous, visible, and posted in key locations.

Print advertising.
Running an advertisement in the regional papers ensures that news of your event will reach many people, even if you cannot get actual newspaper coverage. Attached you will find average advertisement rates and sizes, as well as contact names at the local papers.

The campus calendar.
Free online advertising for the campus community is available on the campus calendar. You can post an announcement or event yourself at CALENDAR.SOU.EDU/.

Web site posting.
You may post an event on your department home page and link it to the SOU home page. Call Curt Whittaker at 552-6956 for more information.

Use the airwaves.
Call Jefferson Public Radio or other radio stations in the Rogue Valley and ask about public service announcements. Some stations provide this service for free.

The Chamber of Commerce Newsletter.
The Chamber produces a monthly newsletter with a circulation of over 800. Placing an insert in this newsletter ensures high visibility. Contact Mary Pat Parker at 482-3486, ext. 14 for more information.

The hit list.
Marketing and Public Relations is currently developing a list of contacts at other campuses and in the community to allow for easier information distribution. Until that list is completed, come and meet with us to brainstorm a personalized hit list to suit your needs.

Follow-up.
The time to follow up on all of your efforts is several days before the event. Make yourself available for inquiries, talk up the town, remind key sources, and enlist student help in driving your message home. Handing out mini flier cards or simply double-checking the visibility of your event information on campus are both simple ways to follow up.

Should the Media Come a Calling

As part of our relationship with the press, we are responsible for responding to their requests for assistance with stories, finding information sources, and clarifying University news. Due to their familiarity with the University and its operations, some journalists may take it upon themselves to call you without first contacting our office. The following guidelines are designed to clarify dealings with reporters.

- If you receive a call from a reporter, regardless of whether you choose to interview with them, please let us know. It is vital to the University that we be kept up-to-date on all facets of media activity on campus.

- You never have to talk to a reporter if you don't want to. Although it benefits the University and your department to have a range of experts appearing in the press on a regular basis, some people are not comfortable talking to reporters. Most journalists are respectful of this position. However, if you receive a call from a reporter and you are unavailable for an interview, it is imperative that you either call the reporter and inform them of your situation or call the Office of Marketing and Public Relations so we can contact the reporter. This is an important courtesy that journalists greatly appreciate.

3

When You're Talking to a Reporter

Request the reporter's name and news organization, then ask exactly how you can help him or her.

Are you the appropriate spokesperson? Do you have authority to speak about the subject? If not, refer the reporter to Marketing and Public Relations.

If you are not prepared to speak with the reporter, write down what they are requesting and ask if you can call them back. Once you hang up, compose yourself, find figures and statistics to make your point, and read through the media guidelines and call our office for assistance. Be sure to call the reporter within your designated time frame.

Understand that reporters are usually working on a deadline. Find out what kind of deadline that reporter is facing. If you need to collect your thoughts and the reporter's deadline allows it, offer to call back later at a specific time.

Be friendly, but assume that anything you say to a reporter will be used in a story.

Ask for clarification if you don't understand a question. If you don't have the answer, say so.

Anticipate tough questions. Conflict is news, routine isn't. Sometimes reporters will frame their questions to bring out the conflict in a story. State your position in positive terms. Don't fan controversy. Don't repeat any negative words in the reporter's questions.

Avoid saying "no comment." Doing so implies that you're trying to hide something. Instead, if you cannot or choose not to answer, explain briefly. "It is our policy not to discuss personnel issues," or "I can't answer that because I haven't seen the report you're referring to."

If a reporter is calling about a negative story regarding the University, please do not comment and immediately contact Marketing and Public Relations. The correct response to a negative inquiry would be, "I am not the appropriate person authorized to speak on this topic. I would prefer that you contact Marketing and Public Relations."

Don't expect to see the story before it's published. Encourage the reporter to give you a follow-up call for clarification or if more information is needed. Similarly, you can call with additional information if you forgot to make an important point.

Ask the reporter to identify you as being affiliated with Southern Oregon University. Know that the reason you were called is that you were deemed an important source for the story, especially if the reporter is calling about your achievement or an event in which you are involved. This is your opportunity to receive much-deserved attention and to draw attention to the number of great things SOU has to offer.

Call us in the Marketing and Public Relations Office at 552-6421 when you have done an interview so we can keep track of clippings or tapes of your story. If you have a clipping or tape, please share a copy with us. We keep copies of stories about our faculty and staff in our "Superstar" file for use in later public relations activities.

Above all, have fun! Talking with the media is sometimes nerve-wracking, but it is not intended to be a torturous exercise. And it never hurts to build positive relationships with journalists.

Tools of the Trade

As per our earlier statements, you should consult our department before the release of any information. And, potentially, we will be writing the release for you. However, standard announcements of information, such as those for science seminars, art shows, and concerts, may be issued by the department. We only ask that they follow the general guidelines we offer, and utilize the templates exhibited in the appendix. All information sent to the media should appear on your department's letterhead. Know that our office will only take responsibility for official releases edited or authored by our staff and submitted on our letterhead.

There are several different formats we use for media communication. They are listed in the order of use, from most frequent to least.

The announcement sheet contains calendar items or reminders.

The media update announces an upcoming event while providing more details.

The news release is specific to significant stories or events and provides extensive information and solid support.

The media alert, for which we do not include a template, as only Marketing and Public Relations is authorized to submit a media alert. This is reserved for breaking news with a short turnaround time and substantial impact, such as a crisis situation.

4

FAQs

Do you design the layout/write the story/choose what's published in the newspaper?

Our office has no control over the media and is not affiliated with any of the publications to which we submit information. The only control we exert is over internal publications or advertisements.

Why hasn't my story appeared in the news?

The work of a journalist is time-intensive and information-rich. Sometimes your story will run immediately, others it may take a while. Unfortunately, there are occasions where the media do not run a story at all. The key is to be persistent and not to rely on the media as your only source for publicity.

Why do we have to use templates? Doesn't that squelch creativity?

Every piece of literature we release to the public, whatever the format, portrays the University as a whole. Helping to build recognition and understanding of SOU is a responsibility we all share. Templates bring all programs in to that broader awareness of the University and thus help to distinguish us (and our incredible programs) from other institutions. Most of this "visual identity" that the templates provide only occupies s a few inches of space on a page, leaving the interior open for creative expression.

Why can't you do the publicity for all departments and units?

Our office is like most others on campus, constantly abuzz with activity and work. Not only do we lack the human power or monetary resources to publicize all events on campus, but the coordination of event publicity is best left to those who are actually involved with the event. You are welcome to consult with us before embarking on your campaign, but your firsthand knowledge of an event is the most a valuable publicity resource.

Why do you keep asking for stories?

We have implemented a quarterly query for stories as a part of our public relations strategy. It offers a gentle reminder that we are here and interested in what is going on campus wide, and serves as a call to action for those individuals who have newsworthy items to share. However, we are open to story suggestions anytime, anyplace.

6

Note: Pages 5, 7—9 consisted of headings only - blank for practice sheets

PUBLIC RELATIONS PLAN

University of Florida
George A. Smathers Libraries
Public Relations Plan
2003-2004

June 30, 2003

Barbara Hood
Public Information Officer
University of Florida
George A. Smathers Libraries

<u>Library Communication Strategies</u>
Marketing Communication Plan Work Sheet

(Name of Library)

1. **Introduction** *(Briefly describe strengths and opportunities to build on, problems/threats to be addressed. Why are you doing this?)*

2. **Communication goals** *(The Dream. Big Picture)*

3. **Objectives** *(Measurable. Doable)*

4. **Positioning statement** *(How do you want other people to perceive the library? What should its image be?)*

5. **Key audiences** *(Who needs to hear the message?)*:

   Internal (e.g., staff, volunteers, board):

   External (e.g., funders, administrators, users, etc.):

6. **Key message** *(The most important thing you want your audiences to know, one central message and three supporting points)*

7. **Strategies** *(How you'll deliver the message, e.g. publications, presentations to groups, media, other outreach):*

8. **Evaluation measures** *(How will you know what worked and what didn't?)*

What makes a message memorable?

Exercises: Name that slogan
What should your library's message be?

2:15   *Door prize/break*

2:25   -Delivering the message: Strategies
What do you do now?
What could you do...new, more, better?

-Evaluation: How to you know it's working?

3:00   **3. Introducing Word-of-Mouth Marketing**
Key elements
Where customer service fits in
Building relationships

3:40   **4. What Next**
Door prize
Review next steps
Questions/Concerns
Evaluation

Library Marketing: More Than Brochures and Bookmarks

10:00 a.m.- 4:00 p.m.

Goals   -To introduce basic marketing principles.
-To begin drafting a marketing communication plan for your library.
-To build skills and identify tools needed to help all staff join the marketing team.

Agenda

10:00   **1. Introductions/Ground rules**
What is your biggest marketing challenge?
If you could have as marketing miracle, what would that look like?

What is marketing?
-Basic concepts and terminology
-Style & Substance
-Resources

10:30   **2. Building a Marketing Communications Plan**
-Introduction: Problems/Opportunities
-Goals
-Objectives

11:15   *Door prize/break*

11:25   -Positioning:

Exercise: Write your library's positioning statement.
What is its style? What is its unique selling proposition?

Noon   *Door prize/Lunch*

1:00   Building a Communications Plan (cont.)

-Key audiences (Internal & External)
Whom do we want to reach?
The "80-20" rule

-The message

I. Situational Analysis

A number of issues have been identified and addressed this year and some are included in the libraries' strategic objectives that were formulated in the visioning process during 2001 and revisited in 2003. The Public Information Office has been involved in addressing and implementing several of the five scorecard categories, especially number 5, "Actively promote library services, accomplishments and benefits to the UF community." Key audiences have been acknowledged to whom communications are targeted.

Communications in the form of publications, programs, special events, and news releases have been designed, produced, and utilized. These will continue to be developed, coordinated, implemented, and analyzed as part of an ongoing interactive evaluation program to support publicity efforts in conjunction with the Director of Development towards donor cultivation and to ensure that appropriate donor recognition and user objectives are achieved.

Internal and external non-development promotional and educational publications, Web sites, programs, events, and news releases will also continue to be a focal point to foster relations between staff members and between the libraries and external audiences.

Public relations strategies will be evaluated on an ongoing basis to monitor effectiveness; and adjustments will be implemented accordingly.

II. Strategy

Using ongoing research, information and data to identify target audiences, monitor needs of individual libraries and departments, as well as the Smathers Libraries as a whole, the strategy will determine the libraries' outreach and education strengths and weaknesses then aggressively and continuously move forward.

Integrated communications is the key to the success of academic institutions as it is for Fortune 100 companies. The fidelity and coherence of the message can be obtained when each component of the libraries' communications is in tune. Promotional campaigns can expect success by involving the complete spectrum of communications including public relations, marketing, and advertising in print and electronic form.

Target audiences: The ongoing process of identifying, locating, and communicating with the various publics will be accomplished in a coordinated effort with the development officer, library administration, faculty, and staff.

Consistency: The libraries' message must repeatedly support the libraries' mission at every opportunity.

III.   Goals and Objectives

Goals represent how the strategy will be implemented. Goals, which are broad in scope, provide clear-cut directives regarding the mission of the communications function. Objectives are measurable steps designed to support goals. Tactics are the technique used to meet objectives.

Goal 1
Develop and coordinate library information programs and communications, ensuring the libraries' identification under university guidelines so that audiences will be knowledgeable and aware of the library services, activities and issues, and will strongly support the libraries as a vital university institution with a highly visible presence

Objective 1
Ensure high standards in printed, online, and personal communication that exhibit consistency for identify recognition and and seek ways to keep the library in the forefront of the minds of students, faculty, and staff

Tactics
Work closely with the libraries' development officer, library administration, library faculty and staff, Office of News and Public Affairs, the University of Florida Foundation, Inc., Facilities Department, and outside printing companies to produce and distribute to targeted publics printed materials to showcase the libraries and/or feature collections, programs, needs, activities, and achievements

Research and write articles and news releases to send to mass media featuring and/or announcing newsworthy items or events

Develop Public Information Office Web pages featuring news releases and online versions of Chapter One, Howe Society and Library News newsletters

Produce brochures describing different ways to give to the libraries for the development officer who will use in contacts with potential donors

Serve on library and campus committees and represent the libraries in the University of Florida Communications Network

Identify and initiate new partnerships with other university departments or organizations that offer coordinated publicity and communications opportunities through association

Work with publicity committee on coordination of Library News, weekly news videos, myUFL, online *Digest* and other outlets of communication to the university community

Special efforts will be made to identify departments within the libraries that receive little public recognition and find ways to promote them by informing, educating, and creating public interest

Continue to notify departments, branch libraries, and committees that the Public Information Officer can assist them with their communication and promotional tools design and production including brochures, flyers, posters, display materials, invitations, handouts, bookmarks, news releases, etc.

Objective 2
Grasp opportunities to help with promotional, educational, and social events in conjunction with specific development efforts, campaigns, or academic events

Tactics
In collaboration with the director of development and library directors, plan events to meet the above objective such as the Howe Society annual dinner and holiday reception, exhibits, speaker programs, social and educational events

Serve on library committees to assist with planning and organizing library or campus promotional campaigns or events to ensure promotional materials are consistent with library goals

Goal II

Ensure that appropriate donor recognition objectives are achieved

Objective
Help bring donors recognition and emphasize that their donation will benefit so many thus creating a legacy for scholars of generations to come

Tactics
Send news releases and photos to the Office of News and Public Affairs to disseminate and/or send from the PIO office directly to the media at the university, locally, in donors' hometown newspapers, statewide and national library organizations as appropriate

Feature donations in libraries' publications such as Chapter One, targeted to other donors/potential donors; also feature on future Development Web site

Assist director of development and program assistant in coordinating and planning receptions, dinners, special events, and gifts of appreciation to honor donors

Goal III

Capitalize on the libraries' addition and renovation plans to create awareness of the ways the libraries are striving to meet users' needs, the libraries' importance to the university community, and commitment to the University of Florida's drive to be a top research university

Objective
Present the addition and renovation of Library West and department moves in a positive light by demonstrating how it will help UF by creating a library system worthy of a top university

Tactics

Keep the construction Web site up-to-date with important information and photographs

Send notices, news releases, articles to the media explaining the process as Library West is closed for two years to address problems with positive solutions to alleviate students' and faculty's concerns

Work with director of development to create and promote naming opportunities for the new addition and renovation

Plan a dedication ceremony with the President's office for the addition, inviting university, city, county, and state officials plus the media to attend

Library PR Initiatives
2003-04

Other PR-related activities & ideas

Announcements – plan and agree on frequency, medium, content

Name the new media room in the basement?
CinemaGIGS
Movie Zone
Movie Den
Films Unlimited
Video Café
CinemaTherapy
Other concepts/words: visual, edutainment, "room with a view"

Signage
New holders (temporary, low-cost "face lift")
Sandwich board out front (balloons, color, etc.)

Food/cookies in the lobby

Guides
– Directory/stand-up map – physical and on web site ("You are here" and/or "Looking for ___? Here's how to get there/find it.")
– Self-guided intro to changes in periodicals location & access
– On-call tour guide

TV in the lobby

Display introducing library staff

Logo contest for the library's new vision

Promotional items (our supply of highlighters is dwindling, and it's time for something new anyway)

Book/video display ideas
– Staff picks
– Student worker picks
– Faculty picks: What I read over vacation

Promote new books by highlighting individual titles in *Communicator, Record, FSB*, library web site, etc.

Student worker involvement
– "Working in the library is a classy GIG"

Additional presentation ideas:

Library PR Initiatives
2003-04

- "Reality show"
- Literary songs

Book Club

"Ads" on library home page – banner ads, scrolling message, pictures, footage

Library PR Initiatives
2003-04

Possibilities for discussion/decision

Date(s)	Idea	Notes
Oct 4-?	Alumni in libraries display	Lisa GC was planning to do something but may not be able to put it together in time for Alumni Weekend
Nov	Anne Hostetler's book release	
Later this fall?	Ariel/enhancements to ILL	
Later this fall?	"Grand opening" for media room and PC lab	• Could partner with ITS for the PC lab celebration (Michael Sherer has already expressed interest in this) • Media room ideas: − prizes to the person who checks out every "n^{th}" video or DVD − "dinner and a movie" − film & lecture (book vs. movie)
Later this fall?	Introduce Library strategic plan and long-range space plan to campus	Must be a multi-part effort geared toward several different "audiences" – students, PC, teaching faculty, College Relations, etc. (Tagline: "Just wait 'til we get some money!")
Later this fall?	Invite the President & Provost (maybe the whole PC) into the library for a special event/coffee break	Could be tied into the strategic plan introduction efforts
Dec	Christmas (tree/decorations/holiday reading suggestions)	
Dec	"Stress relief," study break, or other special service related to exam time	

Library PR Initiatives
2003-04

Date(s)	Idea	Notes
Jan 19	Martin Luther King Jr.'s Birthday	
February	Black History Month	
March 1-5	National Foreign Language Week	This is the week of Spring break
March	Women's History Month	
March	Disability Awareness Month	
March/April	Ex Libris/Aleph	
April	National Poetry Month	
April 18-24	National Library Week	
Ongoing?	Promoting new databases	Could be rolled into Ex Libris/Aleph introduction
Ongoing?	Special "coffee breaks" in the library for various departments/schools/new faculty	
Ongoing?	Regular section in the *Record*	Ideas: • Guest book/video reviews • New at the library

Library PR Initiatives 2003-04

Date(s)	Event	Display			
		Periodicals Room	Lobby	3-pt board LEFT	3-pt board RIGHT
Sept			What's New in the Library (Lisa GC)		
Sept			Peace resources (Anne)		
Sept			Colombia (Anne)		
Sept				J. Denny Weaver's forthcoming book (Anne)	
Sept		*World Press Review*/featured periodical (Sue)			
Sept 16	GC Journal interview (Lisa GC)				
Sept 17	Library Convo: What Have We Done for You Lately? GOOD News from the Library (Lisa GC)				
Sept 26	Celebration of faculty tenure & promotions (Sally Jo)				
Sept 29 – midterm			Faculty book selections (Sally Jo)		
Oct 4	Partners for Learning "scavenger hunt" & literature presentation (Lisa GC)				

Library PR Initiatives
2003-04

Date(s)	Event	Periodicals Room	Display		
			Lobby	3-pt board LEFT	3-pt board RIGHT
Oct		Downbeat/featured periodical (Sue)			
After midterm thru Thanksgiving			ILL (Laura & Sarah)		
Oct 28 – mid-Nov				Li-Young Lee, visiting poet (Anne)	
Nov		The Advocate (tent.)/featured periodical (Sue)			
Mid Nov to end of term				"Introducing Your Library Staff" (Lisa & Sue)	
Thanksgiving - Christmas			Stress Relief (Lisa F & Darlene)		
Thanksgiving - Christmas			Upstairs Lounge: Christmas tree in the window (Kathy & Laura)		
Dec		Featured periodical (Sue)			
Dec		Carolers in the case (Kathy)			
Dec				Santa's List	

Per Oct. 7 planning meeting:

- "New Books" cart will be placed in PC bay on a trial basis (Lisa F & Darlene).
- Kathy will put together a tentative plan for "Dinner & Movie" (this semester or next).
- Anne will contact Michael Sherer about an ITS/Library "grand opening" celebration for the PC Lab.

STRATEGIC PLANS

April 23, 2003

TO: RAL Staff

FROM: Strategies & Assessment Committee
(formerly the Mission & Vision Committee)

As I mentioned in the last staff meeting, we have revised our Vision Strategies to include a way of measuring our progress and have adapted the format used by the Association of College and Research Libraries. We don't believe that the essence of our strategies has changed.

Here is the draft of the new document, along with details on the first 3 strategies we will tackle: Anticipate user needs and promote services, Teach Info Literacy, and Build & maintain resources.

We don't have a team yet for the "Anticipate user needs and promote services..." strategy. **If you would like to participate** in that one, please contact Jennifer.

In addition, Michael has obtained peer comparison data for us which is contained in the last 2 sheets. *(not included)*

If you have feedback or questions on the attached, please let any of us know. Thank you.

Debra
Mary
Jennifer
Lauralee
Gerry
Michael

Creighton University Reinert Alumni Library

Strategies and Assessment
Spring 2003

Mission and Vision

The library's *mission statement* was developed by a staff committee and approved by the entire staff:

> The mission of Reinert Alumni Library is to provide the services and resources necessary to meet the research and information needs of the Creighton University community. The Library staff augments the educational mission of the University by:
>
> ♦ Developing a collection of diverse and scholarly resources
> ♦ Providing the tools and technology that connect people to ideas and information
> ♦ Teaching information and research skills

The library's *vision statement* is for the next 5 years and was developed by the entire staff:

> The Reinert Alumni Library provides personal service to the individual in a state of the art learning environment. Everything the library has to offer, its facilities, information resources, services, and staff, is recognized as a key component in achieving academic success.

Points of Comparison

Our peer group for the purpose of comparisons includes: xxx, yyy, zzz

Suggested Points of comparison: Input measures

- Ratio of volumes to combined total student (undergraduate and graduate) and faculty FTE.
- Ratio of volumes added per year to combined total student and faculty FTE.
- Ratio of material/information resource expenditures to combined total student and faculty FTE.

Percent of total library budget expended in the following three categories:

1. Materials/information resources, subdivided by print, microform, and electronic.
2. Staff (including the head librarian, full and part-time staff, and student assistant expenditures --- including federal contributions, if any, and outsourcing costs). When determining staff expenditures care should be taken to consider comparable staff (i.e., including or excluding media, systems or development staff) and fringe benefits (within or outside the library budget).
3. All other operating expenses (care should be taken to include the same categories, e.g., network infrastructure, equipment).

- Ratio of FTE library staff to combined student and faculty FTE.
- Ratio of library space (in square feet) to combined student and faculty FTE.
- Ratio of number of students attending library instructional sessions to total number of students   in target group.(3)

- Ratio of library seating to combined student and faculty FTE.(4)
- Ratio of computer workstations to combined student and faculty FTE (consider that college requirements for student ownership of desktop or laptop computers could affect the need for work stations within the library).

Suggested Points of comparison: Output measures

- Ratio of circulation (excluding reserve) to combined student and faculty FTE.
- Ratio of interlibrary loan requests to combined student and faculty FTE (could be divided between photocopies and books).
- Ratio of interlibrary loan lending to borrowing.
- Interlibrary loan/document delivery borrowing turnaround time, fill rate, and unit cost.
- Interlibrary loan/document delivery lending turnaround time, fill rate, and unit cost.
- Ratio of reference questions (sample week) to combined student and faculty FTE.
- Reserves – paper and electronic

Strategies and Outcomes

Our strategies and action plans were developed to help us achieve our vision within a 5 year timeframe. These plans are outlined in the attached tables, along with assessment methods and outcomes. The items below highlight some of our completed actions and outcomes.

Services: Anticipate user needs, promote services and collections, and be sensitive to a diverse clientele (Table 1) (Jennifer will do draft)

Objective: What did we want to accomplish
Library Actions: Specific things we did
Assessment Methods: How we measured our achievements
Outcomes: What affect this had on our users

Instruction: Promote Information Literacy and lifelong learning (Table 2) (Mary will head team)

Objective:
Library Actions:
Assessment Methods:
Outcomes:

Resources: Build collection excellence and provide quality resources (Lauralee will head team)

Objective: To develop, in close cooperation with teaching faculty, strong library collections that are responsive to the curriculum and that sustain faculty research and artistic performance in carefully defined ways.

Library Actions:
- Created liaison program....

- Began a continuous weeding program...

Assessment Methods:
- Levels of satisfaction with collection on user survey
- Compare circulation statistics before and after

Outcomes:
- Faculty and students express high levels of satisfaction with the library's collections. Blah, blah, 97% ....
- Circulation statistics went up 15%.

Access: Deliver information resources appropriately and effectively

Objective:
Library Actions:
Assessment Methods:
Outcomes:

Staff: Develop a skilled and motivated workforce that is aware of and respects the diversity of the Creighton University community

Objective:
Library Actions:
Assessment Methods:
Outcomes:

Facilities: Provide inviting and functional facilities conducive to studying and working

Objective:
Library Actions:
Assessment Methods:
Outcomes:

Communication and Cooperation: Create and maintain regular methods of communication within the library and with other departments on campus

Objective:
Library Actions:
Assessment Methods:
Outcomes:

Administration: Govern the library in accordance with ACRL Guidelines and in the spirit of the ALA Library Bill of Rights.

Objective:

Library Actions:
Assessment Methods:
Outcomes:

Budget: Obtain and allocate finances appropriately

Objective:
Library Actions:
Assessment Methods:
Outcomes:

Anticipate User Needs

Goal	Action Plan	Assigned To	By When	Assessment Method	Outcome
Assess faculty awareness of library services and resources	1. Measure faculty satisfaction with library services and resources	MN	Spring 2001	Faculty Survey	Positive feedback, will repeat in Spring 2004?
	2. Provide orientations for new faculty that include Circ. Services (e-reserves) & Tech Services	MN, liaisons. Deb S., Lauralee, David	August	Follow-up letter/visit to new faculty, feedback forms	Revise as needed
	3. Faculty liaisons	MN, liaisons	Liaison schedule	Monitor # of classes taught and faculty requests	Revise for August, as needed
Assess student awareness of library services and resources	1. Measure student satisfaction with library services and resources	MN, JC	March 2003	Student Survey	Waiting for Dr. Wernig's assessment
	2. Measure usability of library services	MN, SG	August	Feedback forms Monitor student contacts Focus groups	
	3. Measure visibility of library services and resources			Focus groups and JMC341 student portfolio	
	4. Continue to develop relationship with the Creightonian			Monitor number of library related stories	
Assess technological improvements for service innovation	1. Attend IT meetings 2. Liaison for IT dept.				

Resources: Build collection excellence and provide quality resources

Goal	Action Plan		Assigned To	By When	Assessment Method	Outcome
Build quality collections that support curriculum and research needs	1.	Update/rev. Coll. Dev. Policy	LG,DS, SG	2002 & Cont.; (every 2 yrs.)	Compare to previous policy statements & include all formats; feedback; survey	Rev./updated and included electronic resource materials in new policy statement
	2.	Create Electronic Resources Selection/Cataloging Committee	LG,DS, SG	2002 & Cont.; meet regularly	Use selection criteria & compare to peer institution e-resource criteria	
	3.	Implement and increase Approval Plan coverage	LG, Ref Liaisons	2000 & cont.	Solicit faculty feedback	Rec'd positive feedback from faculty; included statements in newsletter
	4.	Allocate "New Course" funds and provide "New Course Title Request" forms (10 titles per course charged to library's "Gen" account as seed funding)	LG	2002 & cont.	Feedback from faculty & receipt of materials before new courses begin	6 New Courses established (Spring, 2003); 6 faculty liaisons responded positively and ordered 10 new titles per course
Maintain quality collections	1.	Implement Deselection/Weeding Project	LG,DS,SG GC (Staff)	April, 2003; (every 3 yrs.)	Solicit feedback; record wdn. statistics	Rec'd. mostly positive/some negative feedback from faculty
	2.	Assess Library Vendors	LG,MG,DS	Summer, 2004	Compare vendor discounts, fill-rate, turn-around time, and customer service	

Goal	Action Plan	Assigned To	By When	Assessment Method	Outcome
Evaluate collections	1. Establish peer group, research and implement Collection Analysis system, i.e. OCLC ACAS	LG, Liaisons	2003 – (Ongoing)	System statistically compares/contrasts holdings of selected peer group libraries by subj., title, & call no.	
	2. Evaluate Circ/Usage statistics	LG, DS, DS	Spring, 2005 (Annually)	Compare SIRSI Circ reports (print)/vendor usage reports(e-resource)	
	3. Check/compare standard evaluation tools and selection lists	LG, SG, DS	Ongoing	Compare lists with holdings (% included in collection)	

TABLE 2

Instruction: Promote information literacy and lifelong learning

Goal	Action Plan	Assigned To	By When	Assessment Method	Outcome
Raise faculty awareness and cultivate collaboration	1. Feature article(s) in faculty newsletter	MN, MP	September	Monitor number of classes taught	
	2. Communicate need through liaisons (see *Liaison Roles* on library intranet)	JC, ND, SG, MN, MP	Per intranet checklist	Faculty survey (March 2004)	
	3. Provide orientations for new faculty	MP, liaisons	August	Monitor repeat/return faculty	
	4. Create liaison flyer	MN, liaisons	August	Compare to JMC 341 student portfolio	
Introduce information literacy concepts to first-year students	1. Customize web-based tutorial (TILT)	MP & team	August	Compile TILT quiz	
	2. Revise information posters and Jeopardy	MN, SG	August	Feedback forms, student input	
	3. Promote TILT to FRS 111 planners	MN, MP	March & cont	Monitor participation and FRS 111 survey	
	4. Provide materials for Summer Preview	SG, MN	March	Compare to JMC 341 student portfolio	
Reinforce information literacy skills of upper-division students	1. Teach course-related classes (see *Liaison Teaching Strategies* on library intranet)	JC, ND, SG, MN, MP	First half of spring and fall semester	Feedback forms, pre- and post-tests	
	2. Provide one-on-one consultations	JC, ND, SG, MN, MP	Upon request	Verbal feedback	
	3. Promote and provide instruction sessions outside class	JC, ND, SG, MN, MP	As needed, on demand	Feedback forms	
Provide teaching and research tools for faculty and students	1. Develop and promote IL Toolkit	MP, JC	Start of each semester	Track server hits	
	2. Develop new template for Subject Guides	ND, liaisons	May	Solicit student (and faculty) input	
	3. Update and develop Subject Guides	JC, ND, SG, MN, MP	August	Track server hits	
	4. Create and promote custom web pages	JC, ND, SG, MN, MP	As needed, on demand	Feedback forms, faculty input	

Reinert/Alumni Memorial Library

Intranet Site--Staff Access Only

| Library Home | CU Libraries Catalog | Creighton University Home |

Liaison Teaching Strategies

- Use Active Learning Strategies:

    1. Structured exercises
    2. In-Class discussion
    3. Hands-on individual or team assignments/exercises
    4. Peer review, assessment or critique of work done

- Provide goals or rubrics to students at beginning of class so they know what will be covered and considered most important. Alternatively, have the instructor pass out the information prior to class.

- Consider creating a web page for the class with links to relevant subject guides, databases, web sites and print resources. Goals/rubrics can also be linked here.

- Find out if the instructor uses a class web page, Blackboard or WebCT and ask that your page be linked there.

- Explore the availability of computer facilities. Many COBA classes meet in electronic classrooms, the English Dept. computer lab may be available, small classes that will meet in RAL may be able to use the public stations, etc.

- Consider using a pre- and post-test with some classes. [Go to Samples]

- Become familiar with the instructor's assignments. Sometimes you can influence instructors to make modifications to make the assignments more "information literacy friendly."

- Use well organized web pages as a promotional tool to faculty.

- Let's all get in the habit of including a brief assessment tool at the end of each class.
  [Go to IL Feedback Forms]

- When feasible, consider using various teaching techniques and tools to cater to a variety of learning styles: paper handouts, online demos, solicit student input during class, hands-on opportunities, etc.

- Suggest "Drop-in Sessions" outside of class if the instructor can't devote a whole period to instruction.

- Promote and help develop the Library Instruction Toolkit.

- Identify core courses in your liaison areas that include a writing or research requirement. Certified Writing Courses are listed in the *Creighton University Bulletin 2003-2004* beginning on page 105.

| Library Home | CU Libraries Catalog | Creighton University Home |

Reinert/Alumni Library	**Voice: 402.280.2227**
Creighton University	**Fax: 402.280.2435**
2500 California Plaza	**Ariel: 147.134.177.87**
Omaha, NE 68178 USA	

Reinert/Alumni Memorial Library
Intranet Site--Staff Access Only

Library Home	CU Libraries Catalog	Creighton University Home

Liaison Roles and Responsibilities

The Liaison Librarians strive to cultivate a collaborative relationship with faculty in order to: 1) promote and teach information literacy, and to 2) provide research assistance. This checklist should be considered a "work in progress" as new or alternative strategies are successfully employed. The level and type of support will necessarily vary by department and by individual. Likewise, the form of communication between the liaison librarians and the faculty (formal or informal) will depend on their relationship and the individual culture of each department.

Month	✔	Activity
January		Seek an invitation to faculty department meetings to offer information and answer questions.
		Invite faculty to link to the Subject Guides from web-based syllabi, Blackboard, WebCT, etc.
		Feature news and information of interest to faculty in the spring newsletter.
May		Remind faculty, individually or as a department, that you are available to provide support.
August		Maintain an email addressbook for your department faculty (ongoing).
		Seek an invitation to faculty department meetings to offer information and answer questions.
		Invite faculty to link to the Subject Guides from web-based syllabi, Blackboard, WebCT, etc.
		Feature news and information of interest to faculty in the fall newsletter.
September		Schedule and conduct library orientations for new faculty in your liaison departments.
		Identify and contact student associations in your liaison areas to offer library support.
December		Remind faculty, individually or as a department, that you are available to provide support.
Year round		Send congratulations to any faculty in your liaison areas who have distinguished themselves.
		Alert faculty to new services and resources (both print and online) of potential interest.
		Attend departmental lectures and other functions that are open to the public.
		Be proactive in contacting faculty to clarify or troubleshoot library assignments as needed.
		Share the results of any student pre- and post-tests or feedback forms with faculty.
		Develop and promote the Subject Guides or other resources in support of a class as needed.

		Watch for faculty publications to highlight in the library display case.
As time		Get to know faculty research interests by examining personal or department web pages.
		Get to know the courses taught in your departments by examining syllabi, Blackboard, etc.
		Consider a brown bagger, database demonstration, or other session of interest to faculty.
		Update and enhance Subject Guides for each department (template forthcoming).

Revised March 05, 2003

Library Home	CU Libraries Catalog	Creighton University Home

Creighton
U N I V E R S I T Y

Reinert/Alumni Library   Voice: 402.280.2227
Creighton University   Fax: 402.280.2435
2500 California Plaza   Ariel: 147.134.177.87
Omaha, NE 68178 USA

Sydney Roby

To: William Fox
Cc: Nancy Magnuson; Robert Welch; Linda Fowble; Sarah Pinsker
Subject: Strategic Planning Proposal

Strategic Planning Proposal
Round-Robin Letters: a digital publishing project

Names: Sydney Roby, Special Collections Librarian
Linda Fowble, Multimedia Specialist
Sarah Pinsker '99

Department: Library

The project we propose has a three-fold objective: to experiment with the technologies of digital scanning, digital photography, and the creation of CD-ROMs; to create an on-line Web-based exhibit of primary source materials from the library's Special Collections, with links to other Web sites of interest; and to explore the feasibility of similar projects to digitize materials in the future.

We recently acquired about 100 "round-robin" letters written by women of the class of 1903, The Woman's College of Baltimore, the predecessor of Goucher College. The letters span a time period of 1919-1938 and touch upon such topics as the suffrage movement, World War I, prohibition, and in general the lives of educated women at the beginning of the 20th century. We would like to create an on-line exhibit of these primary source materials, as well as supporting documents from the college archives such as yearbooks, photographs of the downtown campus and college life in that era, college catalogs to show what they might have studied, and news clippings both from the students' publications and from national newspapers that have been saved in scrapbooks, that reflect the social and political climate of the lives and issues of these women. Music from the college songbooks of the era will be recorded and incorporated into the site. In addition, captions may include quotes from faculty and administration, digital photographs of some of the relevant political memorabilia from the Winslow Collection, and other materials suggested by the content of the letters.

The exhibit should be of interest to students of history, womens studies, political science, and education. By digitizing the documents and putting them on the Web we are ensuring that a wider audience than can travel to Goucher will have access to the materials, and that they will be spared the wear of handling and thus preserve the documents. The exhibit will also call attention to the rich history of the college, and to the library's extensive Special Collections. The exhibit will be "burned" onto CD-ROMs that can be shown to alumnae and other interested groups around the world.

The project addresses three of the college's strategic initiatives: it explores the use of technology; it is interdisciplinary; and it is an experiential learning opportunity for the student working with the handwritten letters. That preliminary work is being done by Sarah Pinsker as an independent study in the history department and funded by the Friends of the Library. In addition to transcribing the letters, she will give a presentation at reunion weekend. In this digital extension of her project, Sarah will also collaborate in the creation of the web-site, and write an article for the *Goucher Quarterly*.

The project will be completed in 6 months, and its success measured by the number of "hits" to the website, the number of times the CD-ROMs are used in presentations to alumnae and other groups, and by the measurement of time incurred in the project which will give us guidance for the planning of future, similar projects which will be carried out in the routine functioning of Special Collections and will not ordinarily be dependent on further additional funding.

Sydney Roby, Linda Fowble and Sarah Pinsker will read the letters and work together in the designing of the web-site. Linda will contribute her technical expertise in creating the web-site, oversee the students who scan the materials, and create the CD-ROMs. She'll research the internet to find relevant web-sites to create as links. Sydney will be responsible for finding the archival and Special Collections materials and for obtaining permission from the families of the women who wrote the letters to make them public. Student assistants will scan or photograph the documents, participate in research, and "burn" the CD-ROMs. Nancy Magnuson, College Librarian, will monitor the disposition of funds and as head of the library oversee the project.

Project Budget

Salaries/release time for staff: $2,100 100 hours at $21/hour

Student assistant wages: 500 100 hours at $5/hour

supplies and equipment:
    digital camera 600
    CD-Recordable discs 50

total requested: $3,250

STRATEGIC PLANNING COMMITTEE
PROPOSAL

Name(s) Nancy Magnuson and others

Campus Address Julia Rogers Library

Check appropriate affiliations x student x faculty x staff

Title of Proposal The Frontier in American Culture: a traveling exhibition

Amount Requested **$2,000**

1. What is the project? And what is its purpose? Why is this project necessary? Describe its activities, specific objectives, and desired outcomes. Please include a timetable for the project's duration and lines of accountability (i.e., individual, department, division).

The project will enable the Julia Rogers Library to host the American Library Association traveling exhibition "The Frontier in American History" (see attached) for eight weeks during fall semester 2000, as well as to provide some associated programming.

We will work with the Frontiers program, the history department and with the Friends of the Goucher College Library. Julie Jeffrey has agreed to speak to the Friends next year, and that talk will be one tie-in to the exhibition. We would plan to announce the project as soon as it is confirmed and encourage departments to discuss programming partnerships. Some libraries, for example, have used these exhibitions to develop relationships with local schools and teachers, a possibility we would explore with the education department

We will also use this period of the exhibit to feature related exhibits of materials in the library collection and as an opportunity to evaluate (and perhaps build) the library collection in this area.

2. Among Goucher's six strategic initiatives one or more must be affected. Where specifically does the proposed project fit? How does it advance the college's strategic progress?

The project will foster greater academic excellence by presenting programming that links to the Frontiers program. It will also provide a link with the rest of the campus community through the public nature of the exhibition. I believe this will be an enriching event that will enhance the quality of life for all of us. If the experience of other colleges holds true, it will also raise public awareness of Goucher. In a recent article in *C&RL News*, Gettysburg College reported 6,400 visitors and nearly 400 students who viewed the traveling exhibition "Jazz Age in Paris." Nearly 23,000 people visited the Frontier exhibition at the University of Washington.

2. Why do you think this project is significant? Who will benefit from this project? How will you measure its success? Please be on point.

The exhibit will provide an opportunity to work with departments and programs, especially the Frontiers program. Students, faculty and staff will benefit from easy, eye-catching access to materials illustrating an important period in our nation's history and culture.

Risa Delappe '02, co-curator of the exhibit, will gain important experience in managing a large-scale project.

We will measure success by the number of visitors and by visitor comments, which will be collected in a guest book.

4. Are there any other prospective funding sources for the project? If so, please elucidate.

The library will be contributing staff time to manage the exhibition and programming, as will Friends of the Library.

5. What plans do you have for funding the project beyond its first year? This is an important consideration.

This is a one-time project that will not require future funding. It does, however, fit into the library's ongoing program of exhibits and events in support of the Goucher curriculum.

6. What must happen for this project to be viewed a success by you? by the campus community?

We would have lots of people stop in to see the exhibit and they would enjoy it and make positive comments!